# ORIENTAL
## COOKING CLASS
## COOKBOOK

PUBLICATIONS INTERNATIONAL, LTD.

Louis Weber
Publications International, Ltd.
7373 North Cicero Avenue
Lincolnwood, Illinois 60646

8 7 6 5 4 3 2 1

ISBN: 0-517-05903-7

Library of Congress Card Catalog Number: 90-83422

**Front cover:** Chicken Chow Mein, Fried Wontons, Barbecued Pork, Chinese-Style Spring Rolls, Skewered Grilled Chicken.

**Back cover:** Mu Shu Pork, Indonesian Fried Rice.

CARVAJAL S.A.
Impreso en Colombia
Printed in Colombia

# CONTENTS

# INTRODUCTION

More than half of the world's population lives in Asia. From India and Pakistan in the west to Japan in the east, the northernmost reaches of China to the tip of southeast Asia to the island chain of Indonesia, Oriental cooking offers a variety and diversity greater than found in the West.

Oriental cuisines are as distinct from each other as Italian cooking is from German. Yet there are definite characteristics that Oriental cuisines share. They emphasize fresh ingredients prepared relatively quickly (a reflection on the economical use of cooking fuels), with vegetables often playing a prominent role. Oriental cooks take great care in combining tastes and textures, not just in individual recipes but also in the whole menu. A range of exotic spices and ingredients give both subtlety and excitement to Oriental recipes.

This book offers a comprehensive sampling of Oriental cooking in all its variety, with recipes from cuisines well known in the West as well as those yet to be discovered. Recipes are accompanied by photographs of the completed dish as well as how-to photographs, numbered to correspond to the written recipe steps.

Using the recipes and photographs as your guide, you can easily prepare a complete Oriental meal, composed of dishes from one or many different cuisines. But don't hesitate to try just one or two dishes and include them as part of a Western-style menu.

## ORIENTAL CUISINES

**China** does not really have one cuisine. Chinese cooking includes a variety of regional styles. In the north, wheat and not rice is the staple, such as noodles, steamed breads and dumplings. Flavors are light and delicate, with garlic and green onions adding subtle spark to many dishes. The cuisines of the coastal regions make use of abundant seafood. Soy sauce is the main seasoning. China's inland region is noted for the use of fiery Szechuan peppers, as well as for the popularity of deep-fried dishes. And from the southern region centered in Canton come the dishes most familiar to the West: light, mild cooking, simply seasoned with soy, ginger, sherry and chicken broth.

**India/Sri Lanka** use complex yet subtle blends of herbs and spices for seasoning. Cumin, cinnamon, fennel, coriander, cloves, cardamom, saffron, mustard, turmeric, nutmeg, garlic, ginger,

chilies, mint, coconut, tamarind—these are just some of the flavorings Indian cooks select from and blend together. This is much different from the generic "curry" often applied to Indian cooking. Northern India specializes in oven-charred tandoori dishes and rice pilafs. In the west, rich, mild curries are served. Southern India features many vegetarian dishes that are highly spiced—a characteristic that comes to the fore in the fiery cooking of the island nation of Sri Lanka.

**Indonesia/Malaysia/Singapore** have much in common in their Southeast Asian cuisines. All make use of native spices and other flavoring ingredients, such as ginger, cumin, tamarind, lemon grass, shrimp paste and coconut. Their wealth of spices lured European and Asian traders, who left their mark on the cuisines—most notably in the chilies the Portuguese and Dutch introduced in the 15th and 16th centuries. Rice is the staple, whether whole-grain or in the form of rice-flour noodles.

**Japan** intertwines taste, texture and presentation in their cooking. Japanese cooks have learned to take simple, fresh ingredients and combine them in small, exquisitely prepared portions that please the eye and the soul as much as the appetite. Light soy sauce and a seaweed-based soup stock called "Dashi" are the main seasonings, which are combined with rich seafoods, sparing quantities of meats, excellent fresh vegetables, and rice and noodles. Cooking techniques run the gamut from deep-frying to steaming, stewing to pan-frying to pickling. And, of course, Japan is famous for noncooked dishes— the ocean-fresh raw seafood of sushi and sashimi.

**Korea** is a cross between the cooking of northern China and Japan, two countries that have long influenced its history.

Korean cooking is spicy, with abundant use of garlic and chilies, but there is a pleasing, direct simplicity in the preparation and presentation of its recipes.

**Philippines** is an amalgam of Chinese, Spanish, American and Japanese influences in the cuisine. Different dishes in the cuisine reflect different cultures: Spain in the hearty vinegar-spiced stews known as adobos;

and China in lumpi, the fresh Philippine egg rolls. Garlic is used in abundance, and salty fish sauce is a favorite condiment both in the kitchen and at the dining table.

**Thailand** uses fresh herbs and spices—especially hot chilies—to give a lively flavor to many dishes. Thai curries, frequently featuring seafood, are distinctive for being amply sauced, often with coconut milk. Vegetables are often served raw in spicily dressed salads. Rice and rice-flour noodles are staples.

**Vietnam** is influenced by the cuisine of southern China to its north. Vietnamese cooking is light and subtle and relies on fresh ingredients, especially vegetables. Dishes are stir-fried with less oil than Chinese recipes or are simmered in broths. Fish sauce replaces soy sauce, and fresh herbs, chilies, garlic and shallots give spark.

## TECHNIQUES FOR ORIENTAL COOKING

Preparing tasty and attractive Oriental dishes can be an easy and rewarding experience. There are just a few rules for successful cooking.

Preparation and cooking are two separate functions. Before beginning, read the entire recipe. Prepare all ingredients before you start to cook. This means all ingredients should be measured or weighed, cleaned, chopped, sliced or combined. Many of the cooking methods are so quick there is not time to complete preparation steps once cooking has begun.

Assemble all measured and prepared ingredients in the order they will be added near the cooking area. Assemble all

utensils, plates and paper towels that will be needed.

Timing is crucial because many of the foods are cooked over intense heat in a matter of minutes. Due to the variables in cooking (e.g. type of heat, food, utensil), the cooking times listed in the recipes should be used as guidelines. Recipes cooked on an electric range top may require slightly longer cooking times.

A variety of cooking techniques, including stir-frying, deep-frying, braising, stewing, steaming, roasting and one-pot table cooking are used in this cookbook. Braising, stewing and roasting are familiar Western-style cooking techniques. However, stir-frying, deep-frying, steaming and one-pot table cooking techniques are not usually used in Western-style cooking. The following is an explanation of these techniques.

**Stir-frying** is the brisk cooking of small pieces of ingredients in hot oil over intense heat for a short time, usually just a few minutes. For proper stir-frying, the wok must be very hot. Heat wok over high heat for 15 to 30 seconds; a drop of water should sizzle and evaporate instantly when the wok is hot enough. If wok is not properly preheated, ingredients will tend to stick. The ingredients are gradually added, often being "showered" or "scattered" in from above with one hand, while the other hand briskly stirs and tosses them with the cooking spatula. The ingredients must be kept in constant motion by stirring or tossing vigorously to ensure that every surface of the food is quickly coated and seared with hot oil. This seals in the natural juices and flavorings. If ingredients are added too quickly or in too large a quantity, the oil

and pan temperature will drop; the food will simmer and steam, becoming dry, tough or limp before the heat recovers. Once cooking is completed, the food should be removed immediately from the heat.

**Deep-frying** lends a variety of appearances, tastes and textures to food. The wok is ideally suited for deep-frying; it will maintain an even oil temperature without burning and is deep enough to accommodate large pieces of food. Its wide diameter and rounded shape reduce the amount of oil needed to fry a large quantity of smaller pieces.

Heat wok over high heat until very hot, about 20 seconds. Add the oil to the wok and heat to specified temperature, using a deep-fat thermometer for accuracy.

The key to successful deep-frying is to maintain the oil temperature. Food should be at room temperature; it is fried in batches so the oil temperature will not drop drastically. If the temperature is too low, the coating will not set properly, the batter will become oil-soaked and the foods will become tough and greasy.

When adding moist foods, such as uncoated chicken, or large pieces of food, such as whole fish, hold the wok cover over one side as a shield against spattering. Cooked foods must be quickly removed from the oil with a strainer or slotted spoon and drained on paper towels. Serve at once before the food becomes soggy.

Oil used for deep-frying can be saved for another use. Cool oil and strain into a clean container; cover and refrigerate. Add about

⅓ cup fresh oil to each ⅔ cup of the reserved oil the next time you deep-fry.

**Steaming** preserves and intensifies the natural flavors and colors of foods. The steam envelopes the food, which allows the food to cook and baste in its own juices.

Line a bamboo steamer basket as directed in the recipe; arrange food in the basket. Place basket in wok. Add boiling water to wok, pouring it down the side, to 1 inch below bottom of basket; turn heat to high. Cover the basket. Keep extra boiling water handy.

Steam food as directed in the recipe. Some dishes require vigorous steam, others mild. In any case, it must be steady, not intermittent. If using more than one steamer basket, reverse their positions occasionally for even cooking. Check water level frequently during steaming and replenish if necessary with boiling water. (Steam heat is very intense; protect hands with cooking mitts. When lifting lid, open it away from you; never put your face close to the steam.) When the food is done, turn off the heat. Carefully remove the basket from wok. Let stand a few seconds to allow heat to dissipate before uncovering.

**One-pot table cooking** is a popular Japanese cooking method where the food is cooked at the table and diners serve themselves from the common pot. For one-pot table cooking all ingredients must be prepared and assembled before the table cooking begins. Since the food is cooked quickly at the table, some foods may need to be precooked as part of the preparation. There two methods of one-pot table cooking:

stewing foods in liquid (casseroles) and pan-frying (sautes).

The stewing method heats the food in a simmering liquid that is usually flavored with dashi or kelp. A strong simmer must be maintained for proper cooking. Food is generally cooked in 2 to 5 minutes. Appropriate utensils for this type of cooking include Mongolian hot pot, cast-iron pot, earthenware pot or casserole, flameproof (not ovenproof) ceramic casserole, deep-sided electric skillet, chafing dish or fondue pot. If utensil is not electric, a portable heat source with adjustable heat is needed. If unavailable, recipes may be cooked on the range top and served immediately.

The pan-fry method sautes the food quickly over medium-high heat. A portion of the food is cooked at one time, and as the diners help themselves, additional food is added to the skillet. The food is generally cooked in a short time, about 5 minutes. Appropriate utensils for this type of cooking include electric skillet, chafing dish or heavy skillet with portable heat source, such as a hot plate. If unavailable, recipes may be cooked on the range top and served immediately.

## CUTTING TECHNIQUES
Several cutting techniques are common in Oriental cooking. They are used to ensure proper cooking times and maximum flavor as well as interesting shapes and textures.

**Slant-cut** is used to obtain slices that are longer than the diameter of the ingredient alone would allow. It exposes more surface area for faster cooking and flavor penetration. It is often used with

flat, thin pieces of meat or poultry and long, thin vegetables.

Hold the cleaver crosswise above the ingredient and at a 30 to 45 degree angle to the cutting board. Slice downward following the angle; repeat to cut slices of uniform thickness. To cut very thin, very long slices, hold cleaver at a sharper angle, almost horizontal to the cutting board.

**Diagonal-cut** is used primarily to cut long thin vegetables into oval slices. It exposes more surface area than the conventional straight slice.

Hold the cleaver perpendicular to the cutting board, but at an angle to the food; slice straight downward. Repeat to cut slices of uniform thickness.

**Roll-cut** is a variation of the simple diagonal cut. This specialty cut is most often used on long and/or fibrous vegetables, such as carrots, asparagus and bamboo shoots. Although the angles are irregularly placed, the overall dimensions of the pieces should be consistent for even cooking.

Hold the cleaver perpendicular to cutting board, but at a moderate angle to the ingredient. Cut ¾ to 1½ inches off the end with a diagonal cut. Roll the ingredient a quarter to a third of a turn away. Cut again at the same angle and at an equal distance down the length. Repeat rolling and cutting.

## SPECIAL PREPARATION TECHNIQUES
Softening and cleaning dried black Chinese mushrooms: Place mushrooms in small heatproof bowl; add enough boiling water to cover mushrooms. Let stand until mushrooms have rehydrated

to their original size and are soft and supple, about 30 minutes.

Remove mushrooms from water. Rinse under cold running water, rubbing cap gently to loosen and release any sand or grit.

Snip off and discard the tough fibrous stems with scissors. Squeeze mushrooms firmly between palms to remove excess water that would dilute the flavor of the recipe. Mushroom are ready to use or they can be refrigerated, wrapped in plastic, up to 12 hours.

The soaking liquid contains good mushroom flavor and is sometimes reserved for use in the recipe. In this case, strain the liquid through a sieve lined with a double thickness of cheesecloth. Otherwise, discard soaking liquid.

Softening and cleaning dried cloud ears: Place cloud ears in small heatproof bowl; add 1 cup boiling water. Although dried cloud ears look very small, they swell when soaked and require proportionally much more water than dried black Chinese mushrooms for softening. Let stand until cloud ears have expanded and are soft and springy, 20 to 30 minutes.

Drain cloud ears, discarding soaking water. Rinse cloud ear pieces individually under cold running water, rubbing piece to loosen and release any bits of wood or other debris that may be trapped in the folds.

Drain cloud ears well. Pinch off and discard the hard "eyes" at the base of separate petals or the thick, tough portion at the base of the cluster. Pat with paper towels to remove excess water. Cloud ears are ready to use or they can be refrigerated, wrapped in plastic, up to 12 hours.

Pounding with cleaver: Gently pound with cleaver, smashing slightly. This breaks up the fibers of fresh ginger root, lemon grass and green onions to release the juices.

Place pared ginger slices or trimmed green onion or lemon grass in single layer on cutting board. Tap or pound with a quick, light stroke of the broad, flat side of the cleaver. Use enough force to flatten the pieces slightly without splitting them completely apart. The smooth side of a meat mallet can also be used. This technique, applied with greater force, is used to flatten boneless pieces of meat or poultry.

## GLOSSARY OF INGREDIENTS

These ingredients are available in Oriental markets. Many may be available in the Oriental food section in larger supermarkets.

**Bamboo shoots:** tender, ivory-colored shoots of tropical bamboo plants. They are used separately as a vegetable and to add crispness and a slight sweetness to foods.

**Bean curd:** see **tofu.**

**Bean curd skins:** thin sheets of dried tofu, sold loose or packaged. Store in an airtight container in a cool, dry place.

**Bean paste:** a Chinese seasoning made from soybeans, flour, vinegar, salt and spices such as hot chilies. It is also known as **bean sauce, yellow bean sauce** or **brown** or **black bean sauce,** and is sold in cans or jars.

**Beans, fermented black:** a strong-flavored popular Chinese seasoning, also known as **salted black beans** or **preserved beans.** These are soybeans that have been preserved and fermented

with salt and flavorings such as ginger, orange peel and five-spice powder. Once opened, store in an airtight container in a cool, dark, dry place.

**Bean sprouts, mung:** small, white shoots of the pealike mung bean plant. They are used separately as a vegetable and are included in a wide variety of dishes. Store, covered with water, in the refrigerator.

**Bean threads:** see **noodles, cellophane.**

**Bok choy:** see **cabbage, Chinese.**

**Bonito flakes, dried:** pale reddish-brown, shaved flakes of dried bonito fish fillets. They are used as a flavoring or garnish and primarily as the basis for Dashi. Store, tightly covered, at room temperature up to 6 months.

**Burdock root:** long, thin root with reddish-brown skin, often used in simmered and fried dishes. The best flavor of this firm-textured, mild-flavored root is in the skin. Therefore, only a very thin outer layer is removed by scraping. Once scraped and cut, burdock should be placed in cold water with a little vinegar to help prevent discoloring and to reduce the slightly bitter flavor. Store in refrigerator up to 2 weeks. There is no substitution for burdock root.

**Cabbage, Chinese:** a tender, delicate vegetable with white stalks and green, crinkled leaves. It requires very little cooking and is frequently included in soups and stir-fried dishes. It is also known as **bok choy. Napa cabbage** is another member of the Chinese cabbage family and can also be used.

**Cabbage, Chinese pickled:** types of pickled cabbage include snow cabbage, napa and celery cabbage. Available canned or in sealed plastic pouches. Pickled cabbage comes in many forms including small whole heads, wedges, or shredded or chopped. It should be rinsed or soaked in cold water to remove excess salt before using. Once opened, store in its brine in a tightly covered glass container in the refrigerator for several weeks. Well-rinsed sauerkraut can be used as a substitution.

**Candlenuts:** somewhat larger relatives of macadamia nuts, they are used as a thickening and flavoring agent for sauces in Southeast Asian recipes. Unroasted and unsalted macadamia nuts can be used as a substitution.

**Chili oil:** reddish colored and fiery hot oil made from peanut oil infused with dried red chili peppers. Use sparingly for flavoring. Also called **chili pepper oil** or **hot pepper oil.** Store in a cool, dark place.

**Chili sauce, Oriental sweet:** also known as **Chinese chili sauce** and **chili paste.** This fiery, somewhat fruity condiment is made from red chilies, salt, soybeans and vinegar or lemon. **Chili sauce with soybean,** also called **hot bean paste,** is thicker, darker and may be saltier. **Chili paste with garlic** is similar to chili sauce but is saltier and has a pronounced garlic flavor. They keep indefinitely at room temperature or in the refrigerator.

**Chinese pork sausage:** a rich, meaty, sweet-flavored dried sausage. It is available in most Chinese markets. Wrapped securely in plastic wrap, it will keep for several weeks in the refrigerator or several months in the freezer.

**Chives, Chinese:** also known as **garlic chives,** these slender, flat green leaves give a distinctive garlic flavor to many Chinese dishes.

**Cloud ears:** crinkly fungi with little flavor but a rubbery-crunchy texture that gives distinction to many Chinese recipes. Sold dried, they are softened in water before cooking. Also known as **wood ears, tree ears** and **dried black fungus.**

**Coconut milk:** a favorite cooking liquid for Indonesian, Malaysian and Indian cuisines. Coconut milk should not be confused with the coconut water inside coconuts or with sweetened canned coconut cream. Coconut milk is made by combining pulverized freshly roasted coconut meat with hot water, then straining to remove all pulp. Canned coconut milk is available. Store, covered, in the refrigerator for several days.

**Coriander:** a pungent, aromatic fresh green herb with long stems and thin flat leaves. It is also called **cilantro** and **Chinese parsley.** To store in refrigerator, loosely wrap in plastic or immerse stems in glass of water and cover leaves with a plastic bag; will keep up to 1 week. There is no substitution for coriander.

**Corn, baby:** 2- to 3-inch-long yellow ears of corn with tiny kernels. The edible cobs are slightly sweet tasting and crunchy. Available in cans or jars packed in salted water; drain and rinse with cold water to remove brine before using. Store, covered with water in the jar, in refrigerator up to 1½ weeks; change water every 2 days.

**Curry leaves:** also known as **salam.** These dried baylike leaves give a subtle, spicy flavor to stews. Store in airtight container in a cool, dry, dark place.

**Daikon:** long, white, Japanese radish with green top leaves; it is used extensively in Japanese cooking. Daikon can be mild or hot, delicately flavored or quite pungent. It is used raw—grated or cut into strips—and is also cooked in many types of simmered and braised dishes. The flesh has a fair amount of water, so freshly grated daikon is drained and sometimes squeezed to remove moisture. Select daikon with firm roots and taut skin. Pare before using. Store in refrigerator up to 2 weeks.

**Dashi:** basic Japanese soup stock made from water, dried kelp (konbu) and dried bonito flakes. It is used in soups and simmered foods. Instant dashi products are available and require adding boiling water to the powder.

**Egg roll wrapper:** dough made of flour and water that is very thinly rolled and cut into 7- or 8-inch squares. Wrappers are available fresh or frozen.

**Fenugreek seeds:** pungent seeds that are used to season Indian dishes and used in commercially prepared curry powders.

**Fish sauce:** an intensely flavored bottled seasoning extracted from salted, fermented anchovies. It is used in Korean, Vietnamese, Philippine and Thai cuisines as soy sauce is used in Chinese cooking. In Thai recipes, it is called **nuoc mam.**

**Five-spice powder:** a cocoa-colored, ready-mixed Chinese blend of five ground spices, usually anise seed, fennel, clove, cinnamon and ginger or pepper. It has a slightly sweet, pungent flavor and should be used sparingly.

**Galingal:** used as a seasoning throughout Southeast Asia, this gingerlike root, also known as

**Laos root,** has a delicate spicy flavor. Fresh galingal is difficult to find in the West, but many Oriental markets carry dried slices of the root, which should be soaked in warm water before cooking. **Laos powder,** ground from the dried roots (also available in jars), can be added directly to recipes as other powdered spices are.

**Ginger juice:** extracted from fresh ginger root. Simply grate the pared ginger root, then squeeze grated ginger between thumb and fingers to extract the juice.

**Ginger root:** a knobby, gnarled root with a brown skin and whitish or light green interior. It has a fresh pungent flavor. Store in refrigerator wrapped in plastic for weeks. To keep for months, store in refrigerator in salted water or dry sherry. There is no substitution for fresh ginger root.

**Ginseng:** an Oriental medicinal root used as a seasoning in Korean dishes. Available dried or powdered. Store in an airtight container in a cool, dry place.

**Hoisin Sauce:** a thick, dark brown sauce made of soybeans, flour, sugar, spices, garlic, chili and salt. It has a sweet, spicy flavor.

**Japanese cucumber:** see **kyuri.**

**Kecap manis:** a very sweet, bottled soy sauce that is seasoned with garlic, star anise, salam leaves and galingal. It is widely used in Indonesian cooking.

**Kelp, dried:** black or dark brownish-green flat pieces of dried seaweed. Used mainly in flavoring simmered dishes. To remove sand, dried kelp is usually wiped with a damp cloth before using; the flavorful white powder on the surface should not be rubbed off. Also known as

**konbu.** Store in an airtight container at room temperature. There is no substitution for dried kelp.

**Korean anchovy sauce:** see **fish sauce.**

**Korean red pepper powder:** a seasoning of pulverized red hot chili peppers. Hot chili powder can be used as a substitution.

**Kyuri (Japanese cucumber):** narrower than the Western varieties of cucumbers, it is thin-skinned with smaller and softer seeds. Thin unwaxed European or gourmet cucumbers can be used as a substitution.

**Laos powder:** see **galingal.**

**Lemon grass:** long, thin grassy stalks with a sharp, lemonlike flavor, used as a seasoning in Southeast Asian cooking. Whole fresh lemon grass stalks may be available. Small pieces of dried

lemon grass are more widely available.

**Lily buds, dried:** dried, unopened tiger lily flowers, which give a chewy texture and subtle flavor to classic Chinese dishes. Sold in small handfuls, they are golden-brown in color, very slender and about 4 inches long.

**Lotus root:** a cream-colored, crunchy root with a mild flavor, normally eaten raw, fried or simmered. It is always pared and is normally sliced crosswise. Due to small hollow cavities running lengthwise inside the root, the slices have an appealing, flowerlike appearance. Pared and cut lotus root should be placed in cold water with a little vinegar to prevent discoloring. Store in refrigerator up to 10 days or in a cool, dark place up to 1 week.

**Mirin:** a sweet cooking wine (12 to 15 percent alcohol content), made from glutinous rice, that is used for sweetening and flavoring.

**Miso:** fermented bean paste made from soybeans and a grain malt of rice, wheat or barley. Miso ranges in color from whitish to dark brown. Miso is categorized as **light, white, red** and **brown.** The texture varies from smooth and soft to very firm and chunky, and the flavor ranges from somewhat sweet to very salty. Store in an airtight container in refrigerator for several months.

**Mushrooms, black Chinese (shiitake):** mushrooms with a dark brown outer skin on the cap and beige inner flesh that has a slightly woodsy flavor. The stems are rather tough and fibrous and are usually removed, since they take longer to cook than the more delicate caps. These mushrooms are used for flavor, texture and appearance.

**Mushrooms, dried black Chinese:** these may be used as a substitution for the fresh mushrooms; however, the flavor of dried mushrooms is more intense and earthy than the fresh. The dried mushrooms must be softened before using and will keep indefinitely in a covered container at room temperature. When these are specifically called for in a recipe, do not substitute fresh black Chinese mushrooms or dried European mushrooms.

**Mushrooms, oyster:** mushrooms with a gray oval cap and a white stem. Available fresh, dried and canned, they have a peppery taste when raw, but are mild when cooked.

**Mushrooms, straw:** Oriental mushrooms that are available either canned or dried. They are small and have a long, thin stem with a cone-shaped tan cap.

**Mustard greens, salted:** a brine-cured cabbagelike vegetable sold in Chinese markets. Store, covered with its brine, in the refrigerator.

**Mustard seeds, black:** this Indian variety of mustard seeds is actually a purple-brown color and looks like a large poppy seed. Used whole or ground, they give a pungent flavor to food. Available whole, they keep indefinitely if stored in airtight container in a cool, dry place.

**Natto:** Japanese fermented soybeans, sold in jars. They have a very strong odor and taste and are used sparingly.

**Noodles, cellophane (bean threads):** dry, hard, white, fine noodles made from powdered mung beans. They have little flavor, but readily absorb the flavors of other foods. They are sold in packets or small bundles.

**Noodles, Chinese egg:** thin pasta usually made of flour, egg, water and salt. They may be purchased fresh, frozen or dehydrated. The time and method of cooking varies with the type of noodle; check package for directions.

**Noodles, udon:** cream-colored Japanese noodles made from wheat flour, salt and water. They may be round or flat and vary in length and thickness. They are usually served in a broth or with a liquid dipping sauce and may be eaten hot, at room temperature or chilled. Store dried udon indefinitely at room temperature.

**Nori:** the dark brownish-green, dried leaves of a sea vegetation called laver. Thin, dried sheets of nori are available in packages of 10 to 12 rectangular sheets. Nori is used as a wrapping for sushi and for garnishes. Nori sheets have a dull and shiny side; the shiny side should be on the outside when it is used as a wrapper. Nori is available toasted (roasted) or untoasted. Nori should be toasted before it is used. To toast, hold a sheet with tongs and pass it quickly over a medium flame a few times until it becomes slightly crisp and the color gets darker. Or, in preheated 300°F oven, place nori sheets in single layer on oven rack. Immediately turn heat off and remove nori sheets after 5 to 10 minutes. Store nori in airtight container at room temperature up to 6 months.

**Nuoc mam:** see **fish sauce.**

**Oyster sauce:** a thick, brown, concentrated sauce made of ground oysters, soy sauce and brine. It imparts very little fish flavor and is used as a seasoning to intensify other flavors.

**Panko:** coarse dry Japanese bread crumbs, used to coat foods for deep-frying. Store in an airtight container in cool, dry place.

**Peanut oil:** a golden-colored oil pressed from peanuts that has a light and slightly nutty flavor. This oil has a high smoking point that makes it ideal for stir-fried dishes.

**Prawn crackers:** crackers made of slivers of shrimp and flour paste, which, when deep-fried, expand into large, crispy, almost transparent crackers.

**Radish, pickled:** Chinese turnip or Japanese daikon that has been pickled with salt and sugar and sometimes other flavorings, such as soy sauce or chili peppers. It is bright yellow or orange in color and is used to add a salty-sour flavor to a variety of dishes. Pickled radish is available in long sticks or sliced or shredded. Store, tightly covered in its brine in a glass container, in refrigerator for several weeks.

**Red dates (jujubes):** small dried Chinese fruit resembling dates, with deep red wrinkled skins. Usually sold unpitted and sugared in cellophane bags, they have a sweet prunelike flavor.

**Rice, short-grain:** shorter and plumper than long-grain rice, which clings together after cooking. Short-grain rice is available in supermarkets. It can be identified by the word "Rose" somewhere in its name, e.g. "Japan Rose" or "California Rose." Store rice in an airtight container at room temperature.

**Rice, basmati:** an Indian variety of rice noted for its long, thin grains that have a creamy, nutlike flavor and aroma. Long-grain rice can be used as a substitution.

**Rice stick:** actually thin, slightly wavy, dried noodles made from rice flour. They are off-white, opaque and brittle and are used for soups and stir-fried dishes. They must be soaked briefly in warm water before using. Also called **rice vermicelli.** Store in, tightly covered container in a cool, dry place.

**Rice, sweet glutinous:** a sticky, small-grain variety of rice used mostly in desserts, stuffings and special dishes calling for its unique consistency. There is no substitution.

**Rice wine:** a Chinese alcoholic beverage (17 percent alcohol content) brewed from rice and water. The best Chinese rice wines are well aged and golden-brown in color, with a thick consistency and a rich, sweet, nutty flavor. Store unopened rice

wine in a cool, dry place. Once opened, use immediately. Dry sherry can be used as a substitution, but do not use saké.

**Saké:** a brewed alcoholic beverage (15 to 17 percent alcohol content), commonly called Japanese rice wine. Saké is usually served slightly warm. Small amounts of saké are used in cooking for tenderizing and flavor. Store unopened saké in cool, dark place. Once opened, use immediately. Dry sherry can be used as a substitution, but do not use Chinese rice wine. (In Japanese, the word sake without the accent means salmon.)

**Salam:** see **curry leaves.**

**Sansho (Japanese fragrant pepper):** a tangy spice made of the seed pods of the prickly ash tree. The inner seeds are removed and the pods are ground to a flaky powder. Store, tightly covered, at room temperature for up to a year.

**Sesame oil:** an amber-colored oil pressed from toasted sesame seeds. It has a strong, nutlike flavor and is used sparingly.

**Sesame paste:** a thick, dark brown paste made from toasted sesame seeds. It has a strong, rich, nutty flavor and aroma. Store, covered with a thin layer of oil, in refrigerator. Peanut butter thinned with a little sesame oil can be used as a substitution.

**Sesame seeds:** the white or black small, flat seeds of the sesame plant. They are used for flavoring, coatings and sauces. The black seeds have a stronger flavor. Store in airtight container at room temperature. Do not substitute sesame paste for ground sesame seeds.

**Shichimi togarashi (Japanese seven-spice powder):** a coarsely ground, pungent blend of ground

red pepper (togarashi) and 6 other seasonings. These may include poppy, mustard, hemp, sesame and shiso seeds; sansho; pepper leaf; seaweed; dried orange, tangerine or lemon peel. Store, tightly covered, at room temperature for several months.

**Shiitake:** see **mushrooms, Chinese black.**

**Shiso leaves:** fresh leaves of the beefsteak plant. Green shiso leaves have a slightly minty, fresh flavor. Red shiso leaves are mainly used in pickling plums. Green shiso is a common garnish, either whole or cut up, and is often included in sushi recipes as a wrapper or ingredient. Look for slightly puckered (but not wilted) leaves and use as soon as possible. Fresh basil or mint leaves can be used as a substitution for shiso leaves.

**Shirataki filaments:** gelatinous, somewhat transparent filaments made from the root starch of the devil's tongue plant (konnyaku). The strands resemble pasta, but are not really noodles. Shirataki filaments are most often used in Japanese one-pot cooking. There is no substitution for shirataki.

**Shrimp paste:** a thick, grayish pink, intensely flavored seasoning made from dried, salted shrimp.

**Snow peas:** flat, green pods that are picked before the peas have matured. They add crispness, color and flavor to foods. They require very little cooking and are frequently used in stir-fried dishes.

**Soy sauce:** a pungent, salty liquid made primarily from soybeans and wheat. Japanese soy sauces have a slightly sweet flavor; Chinese soy sauce tends to be saltier. "Light" soy sauce, which is lighter in color and thinner in consistency, is used when it is desirable not to darken the color of other ingredients, such as clear soups.

**Soy sauce, black mushroom:** a soy sauce flavored with mushrooms. It is saltier than ordinary soy sauce and may be slightly sweeter. Black mushroom soy sauce is used sparingly.

**Spring roll wrappers:** paper-thin noodle wrappers used for Chinese spring rolls, Philippine lumpia and other Oriental appetizers. They are available in squares or rounds. Do not substitute egg roll wrappers, which are too thick.

**Star anise:** a licorice-flavored spice that comes in the form of a hard, brown 8-pointed star-shaped pod. Store in an airtight container at room temperature.

**Szechuan peppercorns:** a reddish-brown peppercorn with a strong, pungent aroma and flavor with a time-delayed action—its numbing effect may not be noticed immediately. It is used sparingly.

**Tamarind:** a rich, sharply acidic fruit. It is sold dried in pressed cakes that include pulp and seeds. Before using, the dried fruit must be soaked in water, then strained to remove the solids. **Tamarind extract** is a rich, syruplike product that may be directly added to recipes.

**Tofu (bean curd):** made from soybeans, fresh tofu is pure white and has the consistency of firm custard. The Japanese variety, known as **kinugoshi,** is softer and more delicate than Chinese tofu. Rinse and drain fresh tofu well before using. Store, covered with water, in refrigerator up to 1 week; change water daily.

**Tofu, deep-fried:** thinly sliced tofu that has been deep fried to a golden-brown. Before using,

rinse with boiling water to remove excess oil; pat dry with paper towels. Store, tightly wrapped, in refrigerator up to 1 week. Also called **abura-age** in Japanese recipes. It is usually found in the refrigerator case of Oriental markets, but can also be prepared by slicing tofu to about ¼-inch thick and deep-frying until golden brown. Drain well and cool completely before placing in refrigerator.

**Tofu, preserved:** bottled cubes of bean curd that have been fermented and then preserved in brine, sometimes seasoned with chilies. Also available as **preserved red bean curd.** Store in refrigerator.

**Tofu, pressed:** bean curd cakes that have been pressed with weights to give them a firmer, drier texture, then flavored with soy sauce and other seasonings, such as star anise and five-spice powder. Store, tightly wrapped, in refrigerator up to 1 week.

**Tonkatsu sosu:** a thick, brown sauce made from fruits, vegetables and seasonings. It is used as a condiment with Japanese deep-fried dishes. Store in refrigerator.

**Turmeric leaves:** the leaves of a tropical herb. The roots of this plant are cleaned, boiled, dried and pulverized to make turmeric powder. There is no substitution for fresh turmeric leaves, but they may be omitted from recipes without a significant change in flavor.

**Vinegar, rice:** a light, mellow and mildly tangy vinegar brewed from rice. Do not use brands that are not brewed or that are seasoned with salt and sugar. Cider vinegar can be used as a substitution for rice vinegar, except when preparing sushi rice. Store in a cool, dark place.

**Vinegar, Chinese black:** a dark-colored, full-flavored vinegar distilled from fermented rice and aged before bottling. Italian balsamic vinegar can be used as a substitution for Chinese black vinegar.

**Wakame:** a green seaweed used mainly in salads, soups and simmered dishes. Dried wakame must be soaked in water to rehydrate. The tough center veins or spines are cut away and discarded. Store indefinitely in an airtight container at room temperature.

**Water chestnut flour:** a flour made from fresh water chestnuts, used to give a crisp coating to foods that are steamed and deep-fried. Store in an airtight container in a cool, dark, dry place.

**Wonton wrappers:** commercially prepared dough that is thinly rolled and cut into 3- to 4-inch squares. The wrappers are available fresh or frozen.

**Wood ears, dried:** see **cloud ears.**

# Curried Beef Turnovers

(Samosas)

**Filling**
- 2 cups water
- 1 medium carrot, cut into ¼-inch cubes
- 1 medium potato, pared and cut into ⅜-inch cubes
- 3 tablespoons vegetable oil
- ¾ cup finely chopped onion
- ¼ cup shallots, finely chopped
- 3 medium cloves garlic, minced
- ¾ pound lean ground beef
- 2 or 3 hot fresh green chili peppers, seeded and cut into ⅛-inch squares
- 2 teaspoons finely chopped fresh coriander leaves
- 2 teaspoons finely chopped fresh mint leaves
- 1 teaspoon salt
- ½ teaspoon ground fennel seeds
- ½ teaspoon ground coriander
- ¼ teaspoon ground turmeric
- ¼ teaspoon ground black pepper

**Pastry**
- 2 cups all-purpose flour
- ½ teaspoon salt
- ¼ cup vegetable oil
- ⅓ to ⅔ cups cold water

2 inches vegetable oil for frying

1. Heat water in medium saucepan over high heat to a boil. Add carrot and cook 3 minutes over medium heat. Add potato; cook just until tender, about 6 minutes. Drain well.

2. Heat oil in 10-inch skillet over medium heat. Add onion, shallots and garlic; cook and stir just until vegetables begin to color, about 5 minutes. Add beef; cook and stir, breaking beef into small pieces, until it is no longer pink, about 5 minutes. Add carrot, potato and remaining filling ingredients. Cook, stirring gently, 3 minutes. Cool completely.

3. For pastry, combine flour and salt in large bowl. Stir in ¼ cup oil with fork. Holding hands over bowl, rub 1 handful of the mixture firmly between palms, letting it fall back into bowl. Repeat until oil is uniformly rubbed into flour and mixture has texture of fine crumbs. Add ⅓ cup of the water; stir to mix well. Add as much of remaining water as needed, 1 tablespoon at a time, until dough pulls away from sides of bowl and clings together. Knead dough on lightly floured surface 10 minutes. Let dough rest, covered, at room temperature 30 minutes.

4. To form Samosas, knead dough on lightly floured surface several times. Divide into 16 pieces; shape into balls. Roll out, 3 or 4 pieces of dough at a time, on a lightly floured surface into 5-inch circles; cut circles in half. Brush half the straight edge of 1 semicircle lightly with water; fold piece in half and pinch straight edge firmly to seal. Open dough into cone shape. Place about 1½ tablespoons of the filling in cone, pressing down to remove any air pockets. Brush inside of rounded top edge lightly with water; pinch top edges together firmly to seal. Pinch the sealed top edge between fingers to form decorative fluted or pleated edge. Repeat procedure with remaining ingredients. Let rest, covered with clean towel, at room temperature 30 minutes.

5. Heat 2 inches of oil in large deep skillet over high heat until oil reaches 350°F. Adjust heat to maintain temperature. Fry 8 samosas at a time, turning frequently, until light brown and crisp, about 8 minutes. Remove samosas; drain well on paper towels. Serve hot or at room temperature. Serve with chutney for dipping.

*Makes 32 samosas or 12 to 16 servings*

### Fresh Coriander Chutney
- 1 cup packed fresh coriander leaves
- 2 to 3 hot fresh green chili peppers, seeded if desired, sliced
- 1½ tablespoons fresh lemon juice
- 2 medium cloves garlic, sliced
- ¾ teaspoon salt
- ½ teaspoon ground cumin
- 1 to 2 tablespoons water
- ¼ cup plain yogurt

Process coriander, chili peppers, lemon juice, garlic, salt and cumin in blender or food processor until finely chopped. Process on high speed, gradually adding as much of the water as needed to form a very smooth puree. Transfer to bowl. Stir in yogurt. Refrigerate, covered, until serving time.

3            4            4            4

# Stuffed Bean Curd Rolls

1 pound lean ground pork
8 ounces shelled deveined large
   shrimp, finely chopped
1 can (8 ounces) sliced water
   chestnuts, chopped
½ cup chopped green onions
2 large eggs, beaten
1½ tablespoons peanut oil
1 tablespoon soy sauce
1 teaspoon sugar
1 teaspoon five-spice powder
½ teaspoon salt (optional)
½ teaspoon ground black pepper
12 bean curd skins* (8-inch-square)
1 large egg yolk, beaten
   Boiling water
5 cups vegetable oil
   Romaine lettuce leaves
   Soy sauce for dipping

1. Combine pork, shrimp, water chestnuts and green onions in large bowl. Add eggs, peanut oil, 1 tablespoon soy sauce, sugar, five-spice powder, salt and pepper; mix well. Marinate, covered, at room temperature 30 minutes.

2. Roll ⅓ cup of the pork mixture into a 5-inch-long roll. Place roll on 1 bean curd skin, 2 inches from bottom edge. Fold bottom of skin over filling; fold sides over filling, then roll up. Brush end of skin with egg yolk and press to seal. Repeat procedure with remaining ingredients.

3. Place heatproof plate on rack in wok. Arrange as many rolls as will fit in a single layer on plate. Add boiling water to wok to level of 1 inch below plate. Steam, covered, over medium heat 10 minutes. Check water level; add boiling water as needed. Remove rolls from plate and drain. Repeat until all rolls have been steamed. Cool completely, uncovered.

4. Heat vegetable oil in wok over high heat until oil reaches 375°F. Adjust heat to maintain temperature. Fry rolls 3 to 4 at a time, turning occasionally, until light brown and crisp, 2 to 4 minutes. Remove rolls; drain well on paper towels.

5. Arrange rolls on serving plate lined with lettuce leaves. Serve immediately with soy sauce for dipping.

*Makes 8 to 12 servings*

*Available in oriental grocery stores.

# Chinese-Style Spring Rolls

1 pound medium shrimp
1 pound boneless lean pork
4 ounces fresh mushrooms, cleaned
8 green onions
1 red bell pepper
8 ounces Chinese cabbage (napa or bok choy)
1 can (8 ounces) water chestnuts, drained
3 tablespoons dry sherry
1½ tablespoons soy sauce
2 teaspoons grated pared fresh ginger root
1 teaspoon sugar
½ teaspoon salt
¼ cup water
1½ tablespoons cornstarch
24 spring roll or egg roll wrappers
3 cups vegetable oil

1. Remove shells and veins from shrimp. Remove and discard fat from pork. Finely chop shrimp, pork, mushrooms, onions, pepper, cabbage and water chestnuts using cleaver, sharp knife or food processor.

2. Transfer all chopped ingredients to large mixing bowl. Add sherry, soy sauce, ginger, sugar and salt. Mix well.

3. Mix water and cornstarch in small bowl until blended.

4. Place ¼ cup of the pork mixture evenly across a corner of each wrapper. Brush cornstarch mixture evenly over all edges of wrappers. Carefully roll wrappers around filling, folding in the corners.

5. Heat oil in wok over high heat until it reaches 375°F. Fry 3 or 4 rolls at a time in the hot oil until golden, 3 to 5 minutes. Drain on paper towels.

*Makes 2 dozen*

# Spring Rolls

(Fresh Lumpia)

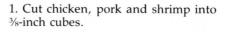

14 ounces boneless skinless chicken
    breasts, cooked
8 ounces lean boneless pork,
    cooked
6 ounces shelled deveined shrimp,
    cooked
4 ounces green beans, trimmed
1 large carrot
2 tablespoons vegetable oil
¼ cup finely chopped onion
3 cloves garlic, minced
5 tablespoons water
7 ounces cabbage, finely shredded
1½ teaspoons salt
¼ teaspoon ground black pepper
1½ tablespoons cornstarch
1 cup chicken broth
¼ cup soy sauce
¼ cup sugar
16 spring roll wrappers
16 romaine or leaf lettuce leaves

1. Cut chicken, pork and shrimp into
⅜-inch cubes.

2. Slant-cut green beans into ⅛-inch
slices. Cut carrot crosswise into
⅛-inch slices, then cut each slice into
⅛-inch strips.

3. Heat oil in large skillet over medium
heat. Add onion and 2 cloves of
minced garlic. Cook and stir until light
brown, about 2 minutes. Stir in
chicken, pork and shrimp. Add 2 tablespoons of the water; cook and stir
over medium-low heat until meat begins to brown, 4 to 5 minutes.

4. Add beans and carrot; cook and stir
over medium heat 1 minute. Stir in
cabbage; cook and stir until vegetables
are tender, 3 to 5 minutes. Stir in 1
teaspoon of the salt and ⅛ teaspoon of
the pepper. Transfer mixture to medium bowl.

5. Mix cornstarch and remaining 3 tablespoons water in small bowl until
smooth. Combine broth, soy sauce
and sugar in small saucepan. Heat
over medium heat to boiling. Stir in
cornstarch mixture; cook and stir over
medium-low heat until sauce thickens,
3 minutes. Stir in remaining garlic, salt
and pepper. Let sauce cool.

6. Top each spring roll wrapper with 1
lettuce leaf so that the leaf covers 1
corner and extends slightly beyond
center of the wrapper. Place about
¼ cup of the filling in center of leaf;
spread out slightly.

7. Fold bottom corner of wrapper over
filling. Fold sides of wrapper over filling to tightly enclose. Serve with
cooled sauce.

*Makes 16 appetizer or*
*8 main-course servings*

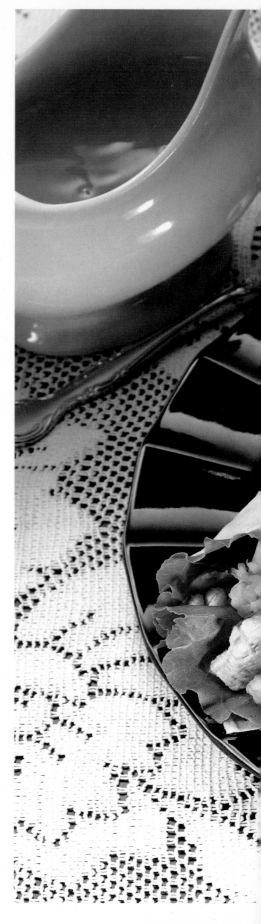

# Gow Gees

Sweet and Sour Dipping Sauce
(see page 31)
1 ounce dried black Chinese
    mushrooms
Boiling water
48 wonton wrappers
    (about 1 pound)
2 ounces shrimp
4 ounces lean boneless pork
3 green onions
2 teaspoons soy sauce
½ teaspoon grated pared fresh
    ginger root
1 small clove garlic, crushed
    through press
3 cups vegetable oil

1. Make Sweet and Sour Dipping Sauce. Keep sauce warm.

2. Place mushrooms in bowl and cover with boiling water. Let stand 30 minutes. Drain and squeeze out excess water. Remove and discard stems.

3. Cut wonton wrappers into circles using 3-inch biscuit or cookie cutter. Cover wrappers with plastic wrap to avoid excessive drying.

4. Remove shells and veins from shrimp. Finely chop shrimp, pork, onions and mushrooms with cleaver, sharp knife or food processor. Transfer chopped foods to large bowl. Add soy sauce, ginger and garlic. Mix well.

5. Place level teaspoon pork mixture onto center of each wonton circle. Brush edges with water. Fold circles in half over filling, pressing edges firmly together to seal.

6. Heat vegetable oil in wok over high heat until it reaches 375°F. Fry 8 to 10 gow gees at a time in hot oil until golden, 2 to 3 minutes. Drain on paper towels. Serve with warm Sweet and Sour Dipping Sauce.

*Makes 4 dozen*

# Pot Stickers

2 cups all-purpose flour
¾ cup plus 2 tablespoons boiling
　water
½ cup very finely chopped napa
　cabbage
8 ounces lean ground pork
2 tablespoons finely chopped
　water chestnuts
1 green onion, finely chopped
1½ teaspoons soy sauce
1½ teaspoons dry sherry
½ teaspoon minced fresh ginger
　root
1½ teaspoons cornstarch
½ teaspoon sesame oil
¼ teaspoon sugar
2 tablespoons vegetable oil
⅔ cup chicken broth
　Soy sauce, rice vinegar and chili
　oil

1. Place flour in large bowl and make a well in center. Pour in boiling water; stir with wooden spoon until dough begins to hold together. Knead dough on lightly floured work surface until smooth and satiny, about 5 minutes. Cover and let stand 30 minutes.

2. For filling, squeeze cabbage to remove as much moisture as possible; place in large bowl. Add pork, water chestnuts, green onion, soy sauce, sherry, ginger, cornstarch, sesame oil and sugar; mix well.

3. Divide dough into 2 equal portions; cover 1 portion with plastic wrap or a clean towel while you work with the other portion. Roll out dough to ⅛-inch thickness on lightly floured work surface. Cut out 3-inch circles with round cookie cutter. Place 1 rounded teaspoon filling in center of each dough circle.

4. To shape each pot sticker, lightly moisten edges of dough circle with water; fold in half. Starting at one end, pinch curled edges together, making 4 pleats along edge. Set pot sticker down firmly, seam side up. Cover finished pot stickers while you make remaining pot stickers. (Cook immediately, refrigerate for up to 4 hours or freeze in resealable plastic bag.)

5. To cook pot stickers, heat 1 tablespoon of the vegetable oil in large nonstick skillet or wok over medium heat. Set half of the pot stickers in pan, seam side up. (If cooking frozen dumplings, do not thaw.) Cook until bottoms are golden brown, 5 to 6 minutes. Pour in ⅓ cup of the chicken broth. Cover tightly; reduce heat to low and cook until all liquid is absorbed, about 10 minutes (15 minutes if frozen). Repeat with remaining vegetable oil, pot stickers and chicken broth.

6. Place pot stickers, browned side up, on serving platter. Serve with soy sauce, vinegar and chili oil for dipping. *Makes 32 appetizers*

1

3

4

5

# Deep-Fried Tofu

14 ounces tofu
1 cup Dashi (see page 48)
3 cups vegetable oil
1 large egg, beaten
½ cup cornstarch
2½ tablespoons soy sauce
2½ teaspoons saké
1½ teaspoons sugar
2 tablespoons finely chopped
   green onion
1 teaspoon pared minced fresh
   ginger root

1. Cut tofu horizontally into halves; cut each half into 4 even squares. To drain tofu, raise one end of the cutting board about 2 inches, using a flat, shallow dish. Arrange squares evenly spaced on raised end of board so liquid drains into dish. Let tofu drain 30 minutes.

2. Prepare Dashi.

3. Heat vegetable oil in wok over high heat until oil reaches 350°F. Adjust heat to maintain temperature. Dip tofu squares, one at a time, into egg, then into cornstarch; pat off excess. Fry 2 to 3 squares at a time, turning once, until golden, about 2 minutes per side. Remove tofu; drain on wire rack.

4. Heat Dashi in small saucepan over high heat to simmering. Add soy sauce, saké and sugar; cook over medium heat 1 minute.

5. Place 2 tofu pieces in each serving bowl. Ladle Dashi mixture over tofu. Top each serving with green onion and ginger. Serve immediately.

*Makes 4 servings*

3

4

5

# Fried Wontons

1 ounce dried black Chinese
    mushrooms
    Boiling water
1 pound lean boneless pork
4 ounces fresh spinach, washed,
    well drained
1½ tablespoons dry sherry
4 teaspoons soy sauce
¼ teaspoon pepper
48 wonton wrappers
    (about 1 pound)
1 can (6 ounces) pineapple juice
½ cup white vinegar
1 tablespoon catsup
½ cup sugar
¼ cup water
1½ tablespoons cornstarch
½ cup Chinese Mixed Pickles
    (see page 61)
3 cups vegetable oil

1. Place mushrooms in bowl and cover with boiling water. Let stand 30 minutes. Drain and squeeze out excess water.

2. Finely chop pork, spinach and mushrooms with cleaver, sharp knife or food processor. Transfer chopped foods to large bowl. Add sherry, 2 teaspoons of the soy sauce and the pepper. Mix well.

**3**

3. Spoon a rounded teaspoon of mixture onto center of each wonton wrapper. (To avoid excessive drying, work with about 12 wrappers at a time.)

4. Gather edges of wrapper around filling, pressing firmly at top to seal.

**4**

5. Combine pineapple juice, vinegar, catsup, sugar and remaining 2 teaspoons soy sauce in small saucepan. Bring to boil. Blend water and cornstarch. Stir into pineapple mixture. Reduce heat; cook and stir 3 minutes. Stir in Chinese Mixed Pickles. Keep warm.

6. Heat oil in wok over medium-high heat until it reaches 375°F. Fry 8 to 10 wontons at a time in hot oil until golden, 2 to 3 minutes. Drain on paper towels. To serve, pour pineapple mixture over wontons.

*Makes 4 dozen*

**6**

# Barbecued Pork

2 whole pork tenderloins
   (about 12 ounces each)
¼ cup soy sauce
2 tablespoons dry red wine
1 tablespoon brown sugar
1 tablespoon honey
2 teaspoons red food coloring
   (optional)
½ teaspoon ground cinnamon
1 clove garlic, crushed through
   press
1 green onion, cut in half
   Green Onion Curls* (optional)

1. Remove and discard fat from meat.

2. Combine soy sauce, wine, sugar, honey, food coloring, cinnamon, garlic and onion in large bowl. Add pork, turning tenderloins to coat completely. Cover and let stand at room temperature 1 hour or refrigerate overnight, turning occasionally.

3. Drain pork, reserving marinade. Place pork on rack over baking pan.

4. Bake in preheated 350°F oven until done, about 45 minutes. Turn and baste frequently during baking.

5. Remove pork from oven. Cool. Cut into diagonal slices. Garnish with Green Onion Curls.
   *Makes about 8 appetizer servings*

*To make Green Onion Curls, cut off bulb where stem begins to turn green. Trim onion to a length of about 4 inches by cutting off tops. Using sharp scissors, cut each top section into long, thin strips down to beginning of stem. Place cut onions into a bowl of ice water and place in refrigerator until onion curls, about 1 hour. Drain and use as garnish.

# Ham and Chicken Rolls

2 whole chicken breasts
½ teaspoon salt
¼ teaspoon pepper
¼ teaspoon five-spice powder
⅛ teaspoon garlic powder
4 slices cooked ham
    (about 1 ounce each)
1 large egg, beaten
2 tablespoons milk
¼ cup all-purpose flour
4 spring roll or egg roll wrappers
3 cups vegetable oil

1. Remove skin from chicken and discard. Cut breasts in half. Remove and discard bones. Pound chicken until very thin using a mallet or rolling pin.

2. Combine salt, pepper, five-spice powder and garlic powder. Sprinkle about ¼ teaspoon of the mixture evenly over each flattened chicken piece.

3. Tightly roll up each ham slice and place on top of a chicken piece. Roll chicken around ham, tucking in ends.

4. Combine egg and milk in shallow dish. Coat each chicken piece lightly with flour, then dip into egg-milk mixture. Place each piece diagonally onto a spring roll wrapper. Roll up securely, folding in the ends. Brush the end corner with egg mixture and pinch to seal.

5. Heat oil in wok over high heat until it reaches 375°F. Fry rolls in the hot oil until golden and chicken is completely cooked, about 5 minutes. Drain on paper towels. Cool slightly. Cut into 1-inch diagonal slices to serve.

*Makes 4 rolls*

1     3     4

# Pork and Lettuce Rolls

1 ounce dried black Chinese
   mushrooms
   Boiling water
8 ounces lean boneless pork
½ cup drained sliced bamboo
   shoots
½ cup drained whole water
   chestnuts
6 green onions
1 can (6½ ounces) crabmeat
2 tablespoons dry sherry
1 tablespoon soy sauce
2 teaspoons oyster sauce
2 teaspoons sesame oil
1 tablespoon vegetable oil
9 iceberg lettuce leaves

1. Place mushrooms in bowl and cover with boiling water. Let stand 30 minutes. Drain. Remove and discard stems.

2. Finely chop pork, mushroom caps, bamboo shoots, water chestnuts and onions. Drain and flake crabmeat.

3. Combine sherry, soy sauce, oyster sauce and sesame oil.

4. Heat vegetable oil in wok over high heat. Stir-fry pork in the oil until golden, 6 to 8 minutes. Add mushrooms, bamboo shoots, water chestnuts, onions and crabmeat. Stir-fry 1 minute. Stir sherry mixture into pork mixture. Remove from heat.

5. Place about ⅓ cup pork mixture onto center of each lettuce leaf.

6. Fold ends and sides of lettuce leaves over filling and roll up. Arrange on serving plate. If desired, pork and lettuce leaves may be served separately and rolled at the table.

*Makes 9 rolls*

# Paper-Wrapped Chicken

14 medium dried black Chinese
    mushrooms
    Boiling water
5 chicken thighs
    (about 1½ pounds)
1½ ounces pared fresh ginger root
3 tablespoons oyster sauce
1 tablespoon rice wine
1 tablespoon sesame oil
2 teaspoons soy sauce
½ teaspoon salt (optional)
20 pieces (8 inch square) parchment
    paper
10 green onions, cut crosswise into
    2-inch pieces
5 cups vegetable oil

1. Place mushrooms in bowl and cover with boiling water. Let stand 30 minutes. Drain. Remove and discard stems; squeeze out excess water. Cut into ½-inch-wide pieces.

2. Skin and bone chicken thighs; cut each thigh into quarters.

3. Grate 1 ounce of the ginger root. Combine grated ginger root, mushrooms, chicken, oyster sauce, rice wine, sesame oil, soy sauce and salt in medium bowl; mix well. Marinate in refrigerator 1 hour; stir occasionally.

4. Cut remaining ½ ounce ginger root crosswise into ⅛-inch slices, then cut each slice into 1/16-inch-wide strips.

5. Place 1 piece of chicken on parchment paper, 2 inches from bottom edge. Top chicken with 2 mushroom pieces, 3 ginger strips and 1 onion piece. Fold bottom of paper over filling, creasing edge sharply. Fold sides over filling, creasing edges. Fold packet over on itself. Fold top flap of paper over and tuck securely between side flaps. Repeat procedure with remaining chicken.

6. Heat vegetable oil in wok over high heat until oil reaches 350°F. Adjust heat to maintain temperature. Fry chicken packets 5 to 6 at a time, turning occasionally, until chicken is cooked through, 4 to 5 minutes. Remove packets; drain, standing on end, on paper towels. Serve immediately.

*Makes 10 appetizers or*
*4 to 5 main-course servings*

# Sesame-Nut Chicken Sticks

12 large chicken wings
¾ teaspoon salt
⅛ teaspoon pepper
1 tablespoon rice wine
  Sweet and Sour Dipping Sauce
    (see page 31)
  Roasted Pepper-Salt (recipe
    follows)
4 tablespoons cornstarch
1 tablespoon cold water
2 large egg yolks
2 tablespoons all-purpose flour
½ cup white sesame seeds
½ cup finely chopped peanuts,
    cashews or almonds
5 cups vegetable oil
1 thin cucumber (optional)
1 large strawberry, hulled
    (optional)
3 large fresh parsley sprigs
    (optional)

1. Detach first joints and wing tips. (Retain for other use.) Prepare remaining middle joints. Cut through skin and meat around one end of wing; cut tendons to detach meat from end of bone. Stand wing upright; push skin and meat downward. Insert knife between the two exposed bones; cut between bones to disconnect them.

2. Grasp the smaller bone; twist and pull to detach it from meaty end. Discard small bone. Pull chicken meat and skin as far down as possible; flatten. Place chicken wings in single layer; sprinkle with ½ teaspoon of the salt and the pepper. Drizzle with rice wine; rub over meat to coat evenly. Reserve at room temperature 30 minutes.

3. Meanwhile, make Sweet and Sour Dipping Sauce and Roasted Pepper-Salt.

4. Mix 1 tablespoon cornstarch and the cold water until smooth; whisk in egg yolks until smooth. Stir in flour and remaining ¼ teaspoon salt to form smooth thick batter. Spread sesame seeds and peanuts on separate plates; dust a third plate with 1 tablespoon cornstarch.

5. Pat chicken wings dry with paper towels. Coat ½ of chicken, one piece at a time; dip into 2 tablespoons cornstarch; brush off excess. Dip into batter; shake off excess. Dip into sesame seeds to coat both sides; press firmly between palms. Place on cornstarch-coated plate. Repeat with remaining chicken, dipping into peanuts to coat.

6. Heat wok over high heat 20 seconds; add oil and heat to 325°F. Reduce heat to medium. Add chicken to wok. Fry, turning occasionally, 3 minutes. Increase heat to high; fry until coating is light brown and crisp and chicken is cooked, 3 to 4 minutes. Drain on paper towels.

7. Cut cucumber slices into decorative shapes, if desired. Arrange chicken wings on serving platter with cucumber slices, strawberry wedges and parsley.          *Makes 12 pieces*

## Roasted Pepper-Salt
2 tablespoons Szechuan
    peppercorns
⅔ cup coarse (Kosher) salt

1. Scatter peppercorns in small, heavy, dry skillet. Pour salt over peppercorns. Heat, uncovered, over medium-low heat, stirring occasionally, until salt begins to color and pepper is fragrant, 5 to 8 minutes. Pepper will smoke; lower heat if needed to prevent burning.

2. Transfer mixture to mortar or small bowl; crush with pestle or handle of cleaver. Strain mixture through sieve to remove peppercorn husks; cool. Store in airtight container in cool dry place. Pepper-salt will keep for several months.          *Makes about ⅔ cup*

# Curried Chicken Puffs

1 medium potato (about 6 ounces),
    pared
  Cold water
10 ounces boneless skinless chicken
    breast
1 tablespoon ground coriander
1 teaspoon ground turmeric
1 teaspoon ground cumin
¾ teaspoon salt
¼ teaspoon ground black pepper
⅛ teaspoon ground red pepper
3 tablespoons vegetable oil
⅓ cup finely chopped onion
½ cup water

Pastry
2⅔ cups all-purpose flour
½ teaspoon salt
⅓ cup vegetable oil
½ to ¾ cup boiling water

6 cups vegetable oil

1. Cut potato into ¼-inch cubes; place in bowl of cold water.

2. Cut chicken into ¼-inch cubes. Combine coriander, turmeric, cumin, salt, black pepper and red pepper in small bowl. Drain potato; pat dry with paper towels.

3. Heat 3 tablespoons oil in large skillet over high heat until hot, about 30 seconds. Reduce heat to medium and add onion; stir-fry 1 minute. Add potato; stir-fry 4 minutes. Add chicken; stir-fry 1 minute. Add spice mixture; stir-fry 15 seconds. Add ½ cup water; reduce heat to low. Simmer, stirring frequently, until potato is tender and water has evaporated, 10 to 12 minutes. Transfer mixture to medium bowl. Cool completely.

4. For pastry, combine flour and salt in large bowl. Add ⅓ cup oil. Add ½ cup of the boiling water; stir to mix well. Add as much of remaining water as needed, 1 tablespoon at a time, just to make dough hold together. Knead dough on lightly floured surface until stiff and elastic, about 8 minutes. Let dough rest, covered, at room temperature 1 hour.

5. Roll out half of the dough at a time on lightly floured surface to ¹⁄₁₆-inch thick; let rest 1 minute. Cut out with 4-inch round cutter. Place 1½ tablespoons of the filling in center of each circle. Fold in half; pinch edge firmly to seal. Press edge with tines of fork to decorate. Repeat procedure with remaining ingredients.

6. Heat 6 cups vegetable oil in wok over high heat until oil reaches 350°F. Adjust heat to maintain temperature. Fry puffs 5 or 6 at a time, turning occasionally, until pastry is cooked through and golden, 5 to 7 minutes. Remove puffs; drain well on paper towels. Serve hot or at room temperature. *Makes 20 to 24 puffs or 10 to 12 servings*

# Steamed Stuffed Clams

4 teaspoons peanut oil
¼ cup finely chopped onion
2 cloves garlic, finely chopped
4 ounces lean ground beef
  Dash ground black pepper
8 cherrystone clams, scrubbed,
  shucked, shells reserved
2 ounces bean curd
2 large egg yolks
2 teaspoons pine nuts, lightly
  toasted, coarsely chopped
  (optional)
1 teaspoon grated pared fresh
  ginger root
  Boiling water

Soy-Sesame Sauce
  1 teaspoon sesame seeds, toasted
  2 tablespoons soy sauce
  1 green onion, finely chopped
  1 tablespoon rice vinegar
1½ teaspoons rice wine
  1 teaspoon sesame oil
  ½ teaspoon sugar
  ¼ teaspoon Korean red pepper
    powder (optional)

1 hard-cooked egg
  Romaine lettuce leaves
  Parsley sprig

1. Heat peanut oil in small skillet over medium heat. Add onion and garlic; cook and stir 1 minute. Add beef; cook and stir, breaking beef into small pieces, until it is no longer pink, about 2 minutes. Stir in black pepper. Transfer to medium bowl.

2. Drain and mince clams. Wrap bean curd in cheesecloth; twist cheesecloth and squeeze firmly to extract excess moisture. Discard liquid; finely crumble bean curd.

3. Add clams, bean curd, egg yolks, pine nuts and ginger to meat mixture; mix well. Spoon mixture into reserved clam shells.

4. Arrange shells in single layer on 2 heatproof plates. Place plates in steamer baskets. Stack and cover baskets. Place steamer in wok; add boiling water to level of 1 inch below steamer. Steam over medium-high heat until clams are cooked and filling is set, 6 to 8 minutes. Exchange positions of steamer baskets after first 3 minutes of steaming.

5. Meanwhile, for Soy-Sesame Sauce, pound sesame seeds in mortar with pestle until partially ground (about half of the seeds should be powdery). Combine sesame seeds and remaining sauce ingredients in small bowl; stir until sugar is dissolved.

6. Cut thin slices from ends of hard-cooked egg; cut slices into flower shape with canape cutter. Cut hole in center of each with drinking straw.

7. Arrange clams on serving platter lined with lettuce leaves. Spoon ½ to ¾ teaspoon of the sauce over each clam. Sieve hard-cooked egg yolk over each clam. Fill holes in egg white flowers with sieved egg yolk. Garnish platter with egg flowers and parsley sprig. Serve immediately.

*Makes 16 appetizers or
8 first-course servings*

# Stuffed Fried Crabs

Sweet and Sour Dipping Sauce
  (recipe follows)
4 fresh blue crabs, steamed, or
  ½ pound cooked crabmeat
1 pound lean ground pork
1 can (8½ ounces) bamboo shoots,
  finely chopped
⅓ cup finely chopped green onions
1 large egg plus 1 large egg yolk
1½ teaspoons rice wine
1½ teaspoons oyster sauce
½ teaspoon salt
¼ teaspoon ground black pepper
3 tablespoons water
5 tablespoons cornstarch
6 cups vegetable oil
  Romaine or leaf lettuce leaves

1. Prepare Sweet and Sour Dipping Sauce.

2. Remove crabmeat from shells, reserving back shells. Break crabmeat into fine shreds, picking out and discarding any cartilage or shell.

3. Combine crabmeat, pork, bamboo shoots, green onions, egg and egg yolk, rice wine, oyster sauce, salt and pepper in large bowl; mix well.

4. Mix water and 1 tablespoon of the cornstarch in small bowl until smooth. Rinse inside of each crab shell with cornstarch mixture; drain shells.

5. Fill each shell with crabmeat mixture; sprinkle filling with a little of the remaining cornstarch. Shape remaining crabmeat mixture into 1¼-inch balls; roll each in cornstarch to coat and pat off excess.

6. Heat oil in wok over high heat until oil reaches 350°F. Adjust heat to maintain temperature. Fry stuffed crabs, turning occasionally, until filling is cooked, 10 to 12 minutes. Remove fried crabs; drain on paper towels. Fry balls, about ⅓ at a time, turning once, until cooked, 4 to 5 minutes. Remove balls; drain on paper towels.

7. Arrange stuffed crabs and balls on serving platter lined with lettuce leaves. Serve hot with Sweet and Sour Dipping Sauce.

*Makes 4 to 6 servings*

## Sweet and Sour Dipping Sauce

¼ cup water
1 tablespoon cornstarch
3 tablespoons sugar
3 tablespoons cider vinegar
3 tablespoons catsup
1 tablespoon soy sauce
1 tablespoon rice wine
3 to 4 drops red food coloring
  (optional)

Mix water and cornstarch in small saucepan until smooth; stir in remaining ingredients. Cook, stirring constantly, over medium heat to boiling. Reduce heat to low. Cook, stirring constantly, until sauce thickens, 3 minutes.

*Makes about ¾ cup sauce*

# Pearl-Rice Balls

½ cup sweet (glutinous) rice
2 to 3 drops yellow food coloring
   (optional)
3 large dried black Chinese
   mushrooms
   Boiling water
½ pound lean ground pork or beef
1 small egg white, lightly beaten
1 tablespoon minced green onion,
   white part only
1½ teaspoons soy sauce
1½ teaspoons rice wine
½ teaspoon minced pared fresh
   ginger root
½ teaspoon sugar
¼ teaspoon salt
   Pinch pepper
1½ teaspoons cornstarch
   Boiling water

Garlic-Soy Sauce
   3 tablespoons soy sauce
1½ tablespoons white vinegar
   ¼ teaspoon minced garlic
   ⅛ teaspoon sugar

1. Place rice in medium bowl of cold water. Comb through rice with fingers several times; drain. Repeat until water remains clear. Return rice to bowl; fill with warm tap water. Stir in food coloring. Soak rice 3 to 4 hours, or refrigerate, covered, overnight. Drain.

2. Place mushrooms in bowl and cover with boiling water. Let stand 30 minutes. Drain. Remove and discard stems; squeeze out excess water. Mince mushrooms; spread in even layer on plate. Combine all ingredients except rice, cornstarch, boiling water and Garlic-Soy Sauce in a bowl; mix well. Stir in cornstarch.

3. Shape meat mixture into 1-inch balls; mixture will be fairly soft. Roll each ball in the rice to coat completely; press lightly between hands to make rice adhere.*

4. Place pearl-rice balls in single layer in steamer basket lined with wet cloth, leaving about ½-inch space between balls; cover. Place steamer in wok; add boiling water to wok to level of 1 inch below steamer. Steam, covered, over high heat 40 minutes. Add boiling water as needed to maintain level.

5. Mix ingredients for Garlic-Soy Sauce in small bowl.

6. Transfer pearl-rice balls from steamer to serving dish. Spoon about ⅛ teaspoon Garlic-Soy Sauce over each ball or pass sauce separately for dipping.          *Makes about 18 balls*

*Pearl-Rice Balls can be made through Step 3 up to 8 hours ahead. Refrigerate, covered with plastic wrap; uncover and let stand at room temperature 15 to 20 minutes before steaming. Recipe can be doubled if you have 2 steamer baskets.

# Steamed Chinese Bread

1 teaspoon active dry yeast
½ cup plus 1 tablespoon very warm water (105°F to 115°F)
1 tablespoon sugar
2⅓ to 2⅔ cups all-purpose flour
1 tablespoon lard
½ teaspoon peanut or sesame oil
Lard
½ teaspoon baking powder
Boiling water

1. Dissolve yeast in 1 tablespoon water in small bowl. Stir in ½ cup water and the sugar; let stand until bubbly, 10 minutes.

2. Combine 2 cups flour and 1 tablespoon lard in medium bowl. Rub lard into flour with fingers until mixture has fine even texture.

3. Make depression in center of flour mixture; add yeast mixture. Stir to form stiff dough. Knead on lightly floured surface, using remaining flour as needed to prevent sticking, until smooth and elastic, 5 to 10 minutes.

4. Spread peanut oil in a clean medium bowl. Place dough in bowl; turn dough over. Let rise, covered, in warm draft-free place until doubled, about 1 hour.

5. Cut 8 pieces of parchment or waxed paper, 3½×2 inches. Lightly grease one side of each piece with lard.

6. Turn dough out onto lightly floured surface; pat into ¾-inch-thick rectangle. Sprinkle evenly with baking powder; fold into thirds. Knead, using re-maining flour as needed to prevent sticking, until very stiff, smooth and elastic, about 5 minutes.

7. Roll dough into a smooth log 8-inches long. Cut crosswise into 1-inch-wide pieces; dip knife in flour to prevent sticking. Place on greased pieces of parchment paper. Place dough (with paper) in steamer basket lined with wet cloth, spacing evenly. Let rise, covered, until doubled, 30 to 45 minutes.

8. Cover steamer, place in wok. Add boiling water to wok to level of 1 inch below steamer. Steam, covered, over high heat 15 minutes. Remove steamer from wok. Wait 10 seconds; uncover. Serve warm or at room temperature.
*Makes 8 pieces*

# SOUPS

## Spiced Chicken Soup
(Soto Ayam)

Pressed Rice Cake (recipe follows)
Fried Onion Flakes (recipe follows)
1½ teaspoons coriander seeds
1 teaspoon cumin seeds
1 teaspoon fennel seeds
½ teaspoon white peppercorns
1 ounce dried candlenuts or macadamia nuts
½ tablespoon water
1 stalk fresh lemon grass
1 piece (1×½ inch) fresh galingal or pared fresh ginger root
6 cups chicken broth
1 whole chicken breast (1 pound)
1 teaspoon salt
6 cups water
8 ounces fresh mung bean sprouts, rinsed and trimmed

Sambal
¼ cup white vinegar
1 or 2 hot fresh red chili peppers, seeded, thinly sliced
1 teaspoon sugar
½ teaspoon salt

3 tablespoons chopped fresh coriander leaves
3 tablespoons thinly sliced green onion, tops only

1. Prepare Pressed Rice Cake and Fried Onion Flakes; reserve.

2. Grind coriander, cumin and fennel seeds and peppercorns in spice grinder to fine powder; transfer to small bowl. Grind nuts to fine powder; add to bowl. Add ½ tablespoon water; mix well to form paste.

3. Trim root end of lemon grass. Cut off tapering upper green leaf portion, leaving about 5-inch-long bulbous stalk. Peel off tough outer layers of bulbous stalk. Discard all trimmings. Pound remaining tender part of stalk lightly with flat side of cleaver to smash slightly. Pound galingal lightly.

4. Heat broth in large saucepan over high heat to boiling. Add chicken breast, spice-nut paste, lemon grass, galingal and salt. Reduce heat to medium; heat to boiling. Reduce heat to low; simmer, covered, until chicken is tender, 20 to 25 minutes.

5. Remove chicken; let stand until cool enough to handle. Remove and discard lemon grass and galingal. Keep broth warm, covered, over very low heat.

6. Heat 6 cups water in medium saucepan over high heat to boiling. Add bean sprouts; blanch 20 seconds. Drain immediately; reserve.

7. Cut Rice Cake into 1-inch cubes. Mix Sambal ingredients in small bowl. Mix fresh coriander and green onion tops in second bowl.

8. Remove and discard skin and bone from chicken. Tear chicken into long thin strips.

9. Place several rice cubes and some of the chicken and bean sprouts into each soup bowl. Ladle broth into bowls. Serve soup immediately with Fried Onion Flakes, coriander-green onion mixture and Sambal. Add garnish according to individual taste.
*Makes 4 to 6 servings*

### Pressed Rice Cake
1½ cups long-grain white rice (not converted)
1 plastic oven roasting bag (8×6 inches)
3 quarts water

1. Rinse rice in cold water in large bowl; drain. Repeat with fresh water several times, until water remains clear. Drain well.

2. Spoon rice into oven roasting bag; fold top edge over on itself twice and staple at ½-inch intervals to seal securely. Pierce bag at 1-inch intervals on both sides with clean sewing needle.

3. Heat water in Dutch oven over high heat to boiling. Add rice bag; adjust heat to maintain low boil, about medium-low heat. Cook, uncovered, 3 hours. Turn bag over every hour; add boiling water as needed to keep rice covered.

4. Remove bag from water; let stand until completely cool, several hours. To serve, cut bag away from rice cake. Cut rice cake into cubes or slice thin.
*Makes 6 to 10 servings*

Note: Rice Cake can be served with Spiced Chicken Soup, Spiced Coconut Beef, Lamb Sate, Vegetables in Spiced Coconut Milk and Mixed Vegetables with Peanut Sauce.

## Fried Onion Flakes
**2 medium onions**
**2 cups vegetable oil**

1. Cut onions in half lengthwise, then cut halves lengthwise into very thin uniform slices. Thickness of slices must be uniform so that they will cook for the same length of time and not burn. Spread out slices on paper towels to dry slightly.

2. Heat vegetable oil in wok over high heat until oil reaches 325°F. Adjust heat to maintain temperature. Fry onions, stirring frequently, until light to medium brown, 5 to 8 minutes.

3. Remove onions; drain on paper-towel-lined wire rack. Let cool completely. Store in tightly covered container in refrigerator.

*Makes about 1 cup*

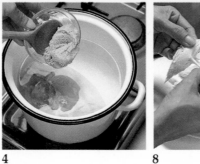
4

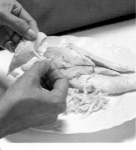
8

9

### Pressed Rice Cake

2

3

4

# Ginseng Chicken Soup

6 dried whole chestnuts
  Boiling water
½ cup sweet glutinous rice
⅔ ounce dried ginseng roots
2 whole spring chickens
  (2 pounds each)
10 dried red dates (jujubes)
6 cloves garlic
5½ cups water
1 large egg, separated
  Vegetable oil
1 to 2 teaspoons salt
½ to 1 teaspoon ground black
  pepper

1. Place chestnuts in small bowl and cover with boiling water. Soak 3 hours or overnight.

2. Rinse rice in cold water in large bowl; drain. Repeat with fresh water several times, until water remains almost clear. If ginseng roots are large, crack with hammer into 2 or 3 smaller pieces. Drain chestnuts; rinse under running water, pulling off any remaining brown skin.

3. Rinse chicken; drain. Remove skin from chicken; discard. For easier stuffing and serving, cut along breastbone of each chicken about halfway up the length of the body.

4. Stuff chickens with rice, then ginseng, chestnuts, dates and garlic. Sew up chickens with large needle and strong thread to enclose stuffing completely.

5. Place chickens on sides in Dutch oven or saucepan that will snugly hold them. Add water. Heat, covered, over medium heat to simmering. Reduce heat to very low; simmer, covered, until chickens are very tender, about 1½ hours. If water does not cover chickens completely, turn them over after first 45 minutes of cooking.

6. While chickens are cooking, lightly beat egg white and yolk in separate bowls. Heat lightly oiled small skillet over low heat 1 minute. Add egg white, tilting pan to form even layer.

Cook until completely set, 1 to 2 minutes; remove to plate. Repeat with egg yolk. Roll up egg white and egg yolk sheets separately; cut crosswise into thin slices.

7. Carefully remove chickens from broth; remove thread. Remove 2 or 3 dates from stuffing; cut into thin slivers. Place chickens in serving bowl with broth; garnish with date slivers and egg shreds. Serve with salt and pepper. *Makes 4 servings*

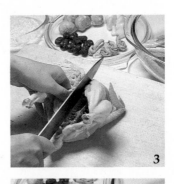

# Chicken and Cellophane Noodle Soup

(Mien Ga)

8 medium dried black Chinese
    mushrooms
    Boiling water
2 quarts chicken broth
1 whole chicken breast (1 pound)
3 to 4 ounces chicken giblets
    (optional)
1 medium onion, cut into quarters
6 thin slices pared fresh ginger
    root
1 clove garlic, sliced
3 ounces dried cellophane noodles
    (bean threads)
1 quart warm water
⅓ cup nuoc mam (fish sauce)
⅛ teaspoon ground black pepper
1½ tablespoons chopped fresh
    coriander leaves
1½ tablespoons chopped green
    onion tops
1 tablespoon chopped fresh mint
    leaves

1. Place mushrooms in bowl and cover with boiling water. Let stand 30 minutes.

2. Meanwhile, combine broth, chicken breast, giblets, onion, ginger and garlic in Dutch oven. Heat over high heat to boiling. Reduce heat to low; simmer, covered, 7 minutes. Remove and reserve giblets. Continue simmering chicken breast until tender, 10 to 12 minutes; remove pan from heat. Remove chicken breast from broth; let stand until cool enough to handle.

3. While chicken is cooking, cut noodles with scissors into 4-inch lengths. Place noodles in medium bowl and cover with 1 quart warm water. Soak 15 minutes to soften.

4. Drain mushrooms; rinse under cold running water. Trim and discard stems; squeeze out excess water. Cut into ⅜-inch squares.

5. Strain broth, discarding solids; return broth to Dutch oven. Add mushrooms, nuoc mam and pepper. Cook, covered, over low heat.

6. Drain noodles. Finely chop giblets. Remove and discard skin and bone from chicken. Tear into long thin strips.

7. Add noodles, giblets and chicken to soup; increase heat to medium-low. Simmer, uncovered, 5 minutes.

8. Transfer soup to tureen. Mix coriander, green onions and mint in small bowl; place spice mixture in center of soup. Serve immediately.

*Makes 4 to 6 servings*

# Hot and Sour Soup

3 dried wood ears or 4 dried black
    Chinese mushrooms
20 dried lily buds (optional)
    Hot water
½ cup sliced bamboo shoots (½ of
    8-ounce can)
1 boneless skinless chicken breast
    half
1 tablespoon dry sherry
4 cups chicken broth
4 ounces bean curd, drained and
    cut into ½-inch cubes
3 tablespoons white vinegar
1 tablespoon soy sauce
½ teaspoon ground white pepper
2 tablespoons cornstarch
3 tablespoons water
1 large egg, lightly beaten
1 teaspoon sesame oil
2 green onions, cut into 1½-inch
    slivers
2 tablespoons chopped fresh
    coriander leaves

1. Place wood ears and lily buds in separate bowls; cover with hot water. Let soak 30 minutes; drain. Pinch out hard knobs from center of wood ears and discard. Squeeze out excess water. Cut wood ears into thin strips. (If using mushrooms, cut off and discard stems; cut caps into thin slices.) Cut off and discard hard tips from lily buds; tie each bud onto itself to make a knot in the middle.

2. Cut bamboo shoots into matchstick pieces.

3. Cut chicken crosswise into thin slices; sprinkle with sherry. Let stand 15 minutes.

4. Heat chicken broth in large saucepan over high heat to boiling. Add wood ears, lily buds, chicken and bamboo shoots. Reduce heat to low; simmer, uncovered, 3 minutes. Add bean curd, vinegar, soy sauce and white pepper; simmer 3 minutes.

5. Blend cornstarch and water in small cup until smooth; stir into soup. Cook, stirring constantly, until slightly thickened. Turn off heat. Stirring con-stantly, slowly pour egg into soup. Stir in sesame oil and onions. Ladle into soup bowls; sprinkle with coriander. Serve immediately.

*Makes 4 to 6 servings*

# Chicken and Abalone Soup

1 pound boneless skinless chicken
   breast
1 can (1 pound) abalone
3 green onions, white part only
3 slices (⅛-inch-thick each) pared
   fresh ginger root
3 cups water
¼ teaspoon salt
⅛ teaspoon ground white pepper
¼ cup fresh coriander leaves

1. Cut chicken crosswise into ¼-inch slices.

2. Drain abalone, reserving broth. Cut abalone crosswise into ¹⁄₁₆-inch slices.

3. Lightly pound green onions and ginger with flat side of cleaver to smash slightly.

4. Combine green onions, ginger, water, salt and reserved broth in large saucepan. Heat over medium heat to boiling.

5. Add chicken; reduce heat to low. Cook, uncovered, just until chicken is cooked, about 3 minutes.

6. Add abalone to pan; cook just until heated, about 1 minute. Do not overcook or abalone will become tough. Remove and discard onions and ginger; stir in pepper. Serve immediately with coriander.

*Makes 4 to 5 servings*

# Duck, Pork and Salted Vegetable Soup

11 ounces salted mustard greens,*
   rinsed
1 ounce salted plums,** rinsed
4 quarts water
½ duck (2¼ pounds)
1 pound boneless pork shoulder
½ pound small tomatoes
⅔ ounce sliced dried tamarind
   fruit***
1 tablespoon brandy

1. Place mustard greens, plums and 2 quarts of the water in large bowl. Soak for 15 minutes to remove excess salt. Drain well. Slant-cut mustard greens into 2-inch pieces.

2. Remove wings and legs from duck. Cut wings into 2-inch pieces. Cut body crosswise into 2-inch pieces.

3. Cut pork into 2×1×1-inch pieces. Cut tomatoes into halves.

4. Combine pork and remaining 2 quarts water in Dutch oven. Heat over medium heat to boiling. Reduce heat to low; skim foam. Simmer, covered, 15 minutes.

5. Add duck, mustard greens, plums and tamarind. Heat over medium heat to boiling. Reduce heat to low; simmer, uncovered, 15 minutes, skimming foam occasionally. Cover; simmer until duck is tender, about 45 minutes. Skim fat.

6. Just before serving, add tomatoes and brandy to soup; cook just until heated. *Makes 6 to 8 servings*

*For a more spicy variation, substitute canned Szechuan preserved vegetables for mustard greens. Rinse vegetables well; cut into ⅛-inch slices and soak as directed in Step 1.

**Available in oriental grocery stores.

***If not available, tamarind can be omitted; add 1 to 2 teaspoons fresh lime juice in Step 6.

2

5

2                     3                     4

# Wonton Soup

½ cup finely chopped cabbage
4 ounces shelled deveined shrimp, finely chopped
8 ounces lean ground pork
3 green onions, finely chopped
1 large egg, lightly beaten
1½ tablespoons cornstarch
2 teaspoons soy sauce
1½ teaspoons sesame oil
1 teaspoon oyster sauce
48 wonton wrappers
1 large egg white, lightly beaten
¾ pound Chinese cabbage (napa or bok choy)
6 cups chicken broth
½ teaspoon sesame oil
1 cup thinly sliced Barbecued Pork (see page 24)
3 green onions, thinly sliced

1. For filling, squeeze cabbage to remove as much moisture as possible. Place cabbage in large bowl. Add shrimp, pork, chopped onions, whole egg, cornstarch, soy sauce, sesame oil and oyster sauce; mix well.

2. For wontons, place 1 wonton wrapper on work surface with one point facing you. Mound 1 teaspoon filling in bottom corner. Moisten top edge with egg white; fold top corner over filling.

3. Moisten side corners with egg white. Bring side corners together, overlapping slightly. Pinch together firmly to seal. Cover finished wontons with plastic wrap while you fill remaining wontons. (Cook immediately, refrigerate up to 8 hours or freeze in resealable plastic bag.)

4. Cook wontons in large pot of boiling water until filling is no longer pink, about 4 minutes (6 minutes if frozen). Drain, then place in bowl of cold water to prevent wontons from sticking together.

5. Cut Chinese cabbage stems into 1-inch slices; cut leaves in half crosswise.

6. Heat chicken broth in large saucepan over high heat to boiling. Add bok choy and sesame oil; cook 2 minutes. Drain wontons and add to hot broth. Add slices of Barbecued Pork and sliced onions. Ladle into soup bowls. Serve immediately.
*Makes 6 servings*

# Pork and Seafood Meatball Soup

7 ounces shelled deveined
   medium shrimp
3 ounces white fish fillet, skinned
2 ounces pressed tofu
9 ounces lean ground pork
2 tablespoons peanut oil
1½ teaspoons sugar
1¼ teaspoons salt
¼ teaspoon ground white pepper
1 can (8½ ounces) bamboo shoots,
   rinsed and drained
4 green onions, white part only
5 slices pared fresh ginger root
   (about 1 inch in diameter)
3 cups chicken broth
3 cups water
1 tablespoon soy sauce
1 tablespoon rice wine
1 tablespoon fresh coriander leaves

1. Mince shrimp; pound with blunt edge of cleaver to consistency of rough paste. Repeat with white fish.

2. Mash tofu in mortar with pestle (or in shallow bowl with fork) to fine paste.

3. Combine shrimp, fish, tofu, pork, oil, sugar, ¾ teaspoon salt and the pepper in large bowl; mix well. Let stand, covered, at room temperature 30 minutes.

4. Cut bamboo shoots into ⅛-inch-wide strips. Lightly pound onions and ginger with flat side of cleaver to smash slightly.

5. Combine broth and water in large saucepan. Heat over high heat to boiling. Add bamboo shoots, onions and ginger. Reduce heat to low: simmer, covered, 15 minutes.

6. Meanwhile, shape meat mixture into balls, using 2 tablespoons for each.

7. Add meatballs, ¼ at a time, to soup; stir gently after each addition. Increase heat to medium. Cook, uncovered, stirring occasionally, until meatballs are cooked, 15 to 20 minutes. Reduce heat as needed during cooking to maintain a simmer.

8. Skim foam; remove and discard onions and ginger. Stir in soy sauce, rice wine, coriander and remaining ½ teaspoon salt. Ladle soup into bowls. Serve immediately.

*Makes 4 to 6 servings*

**1**

**2**

**6**

**7**

# Hot and Sour Prawn Soup

(Tom Yam Kung)

2 shallots
2 fresh or dried long red chili
    peppers, seeded
8 whole fresh prawns or tiger
    shrimp, preferably with heads
    (about ½ pound)
5 cups water
2 stalks fresh lemon grass
2 to 3 tablespoons fish sauce
1½ to 2 tablespoons fresh lime juice
1 teaspoon sugar
    Fresh coriander leaves

1. Roast shallots and chilies in small dry skillet over low heat, turning frequently, until softened, 10 to 15 minutes. Pound shallots and chilies in mortar with pestle to fine paste.

2. Detach heads from prawns and reserve. Leaving tails intact, shell and devein prawns; reserve shells separately.

3. Place water and reserved shells in large saucepan. Heat over high heat to boiling. Reduce heat to low; simmer, covered, 10 minutes. Strain broth and return to pan; discard shells.

4. Trim root end of lemon grass. Cut off tapering upper green leaf portion, leaving about 5-inch long bulbous stalk. Peel off tough outer layers of bulbous stalk. Discard all trimmings. Pound remaining tender part of stalk lightly with flat side of cleaver to smash slightly. Cut each piece in half crosswise.

5. Combine shallot-chili paste with 2 tablespoons of the fish sauce, 1½ tablespoons lime juice and the sugar in small bowl; mix well.

6. Add lemon grass to broth. Simmer, uncovered, 10 minutes. Add prawns and reserved heads to broth. Cook, uncovered, over medium heat just until prawns are opaque, about 3 minutes. Remove prawns and heads with slotted spoon and put into serving bowls. Remove and discard lemon grass.

7. Add shallot mixture to broth; mix well. Cook and stir over low heat 1 minute; taste and adjust seasonings with remaining 1 tablespoon fish sauce and ½ tablespoon lime juice if necessary. Ladle broth over prawns in each bowl. Garnish with coriander leaves. Serve immediately.

*Makes 4 to 8 servings*

# Clam with Pineapple Soup

5 cups water
2¼ pounds cherrystone clams, scrubbed (about 2 dozen)
2 to 3 small tomatoes (about 8 ounces)
1 slice fresh pineapple (1¼ inches thick), pared
2 tablespoons vegetable oil
1 medium onion, chopped
1 clove garlic, minced
2 teaspoons sweet chili sauce
¼ cup nouc mam (fish sauce)
½ to 1 tablespoon fresh lemon juice
3 to 4 green onions, tops only, cut into 1-inch pieces

1. Heat water in large saucepan over high heat to boiling. Add clams; reduce heat to medium. Cook, covered, just until shells open, 5 to 8 minutes. Discard any clams that do not open. Strain broth through sieve lined with dampened muslin; reserve. Let clams stand until cool enough to handle.

2. Cut each tomato into 8 wedges. Cut pineapple slice in half. Cut out and discard core. Cut pineapple into ⅛-inch slices.

3. Return clam broth to clean large saucepan; add tomatoes and pineapple. Heat over medium heat to boiling. Reduce heat to medium-low; simmer, uncovered, while proceeding with recipe.

4. Remove clams from shells; discard shells.

5. Heat oil in large skillet over medium heat. Add onion and garlic; cook and stir until onion is soft, about 4 minutes. Add clams and chili sauce; cook and stir 3 minutes.

6. Add clam-onion mixture to soup; heat over medium-high heat just until soup comes to a boil. Remove from heat; stir in nuoc mam and lemon juice. Ladle soup into bowls; sprinkle with green onions. Serve immediately.

*Makes 4 to 6 servings*

# Clam Soup

(Hamaguri Ushio-Jiru)

4 large or 8 medium hard-shell
    clams
2 quarts water
4½ teaspoons salt
1 piece (4 inches square) konbu
    (dried kelp)
2 green onions
1 piece (1 inch square) lemon rind
1 teaspoon saké
½ teaspoon soy sauce

1. Scrub clams under cold running water. Soak clams in 1 quart water and 4 teaspoons salt in medium bowl 15 to 20 minutes.

2. Meanwhile, wipe kelp gently with damp cloth to remove any sand (but not the white powder) that may adhere to surface. Using scissors, cut kelp crosswise into 4 equal strips.

3. Cut green onions crosswise into very thin slices. Cut lemon rind into ¹⁄₁₆-inch-wide strips.

4. Remove clams from salt water; rinse under cold running water. Place clams, kelp and remaining 1 quart water in 2-quart saucepan; heat to boiling over medium-high heat. Just **before** water boils, remove and discard kelp pieces.

5. Skim foam from surface of soup. Add saké, soy sauce and remaining ½ teaspoon salt to soup. Reduce heat to medium. Boil gently until clams open, about 5 minutes. Stir green onions into soup; remove from heat. (Discard any clams that do not open.) Skim foam from surface.

6. Place 1 clam in each of 4 soup bowls. (If using medium clams, remove meat from second clam and place meat in empty half-shell of first clam in soup bowl.) Ladle about 1 cup of soup over clam in each bowl. Sprinkle lemon strips over each serving.

*Makes 4 servings*

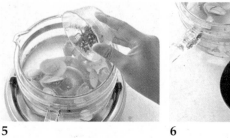

2

5

6

# Clear Soup with Shrimp

(Ebi Sumashi-Jiru)

4 large or 8 medium shrimp, in
    shells
2 pods okra
1 piece (1 inch square) lemon rind
2 cups water
1¼ teaspoons salt
1 quart Dashi (see page 48)
1 teaspoon light soy sauce

1. Leaving tail and section of shell nearest tail attached, shell and devein shrimp.

2. Cut okra crosswise into ⅛-inch-thick slices. Cut lemon rind into ¹⁄₁₆-inch-wide strips.

3. Combine water and ¼ teaspoon salt in 1½ quart saucepan; heat until water simmers. Add shrimp; reduce heat to low. Simmer until shrimp are opaque and cooked through, about 3 minutes. Drain shrimp.

4. Combine Dashi and remaining 1 teaspoon salt in 1½-quart saucepan; heat to boiling over medium-high heat, stirring until salt dissolves. Add soy sauce and okra to Dashi; remove from heat.

5. Place 1 large or 2 medium shrimp in each of 4 soup bowls; ladle about 1 cup of soup over shrimp in each bowl. Sprinkle lemon strips over each serving. *Makes 4 servings*

1

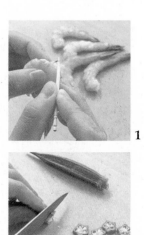

2

5

# Miso Soup with Tofu

(Tofu Miso Shiru)

½ ounce wakame (salted dried
   seaweed)
1 quart warm water
1 quart Dashi (recipe follows)
¼ cup light miso (bean paste)
12 ounces kinugoshi (soft tofu),
   drained
2 tablespoons thinly sliced green
   onions
   Pickled cucumber and cabbage
   Hot cooked white rice

1. Place wakame and warm water in small bowl. Soak for 20 minutes to soften and to remove salt.

2. Meanwhile, prepare Dashi.

3. Drain wakame; pat dry with paper towels. Cut off and discard any tough stems. Cut wakame crosswise into 1½-inch-long pieces.

4. Heat Dashi in medium saucepan over medium heat to simmering; reduce heat to low. Place miso in small bowl; gradually stir in ½ cup Dashi until miso is evenly thinned and dissolved. Gradually stir miso mixture into remaining Dashi.

5. Add wakame; simmer, uncovered, over low heat 1 minute.

6. Cut kinugoshi into ½-inch cubes; add to soup. Cook over low heat 1 minute; do not boil.

7. Ladle soup into bowls; sprinkle with green onions. Serve with pickles and rice.           *Makes 4 servings*

## Dashi (Basic Soup Stock)
   1 piece (4 inches square) konbu
      (dried kelp)
   1 quart plus ¼ cup cold water
   ⅔ cup dried bonito flakes

1. Wipe konbu gently with damp cloth to remove any sand that may adhere to surface. Using scissors, cut konbu crosswise into 4 equal strips.

2. Place konbu and 1 quart of the water in medium saucepan. Heat over medium heat to boiling; just **before** water boils, remove and discard konbu.

3. Add remaining ¼ cup water to pan to stop boiling. Immediately add bonito flakes. When stock comes to a full boil, immediately remove from heat.

4. Let stand until bonito flakes settle to bottom of pan, about 1 minute. Strain stock through sieve lined with dampened cheesecloth; discard bonito flakes. Dashi can be refrigerated, covered, up to 4 days. Do not freeze.
           *Makes about 1 quart*

Note: Products for making "instant" dashi are available. Known as "dashi-no-moto," they come in the form of seasoned dried bonito flakes in large infusion bags (such as oversized teabags), or in granule form, sometimes called "hon-dashi." These products can be used as a satisfactory substitute for homemade dashi.

# Stuffed Squid Soup

6 medium squid (about 1 pound)
½ pound lean ground pork, at
    room temperature
3 tablespoons fish sauce
1½ teaspoons minced fresh
    coriander, leaves and stems
1 teaspoon minced pared fresh
    ginger root
1 clove garlic, minced
¼ teaspoon salt
⅛ teaspoon ground black pepper
6 cups chicken broth
2 medium onions, cut into halves
1 teaspoon sugar
¼ cup sliced green onion, tops only

1. To clean squid, work over sink. Hold body of squid firmly in one hand; grasp head section firmly with other hand. Pull head, twisting gently from side to side; head and body contents should come away in one piece. Squeeze head section at base of tentacles to remove and discard innards and core. Feel inside body for thin transparent quill. Firmly grasp quill and attached viscera; remove and discard. Rinse head and tentacle sections and inside of the squid bodies thoroughly; drain well.

2. Combine pork, 1 tablespoon of the fish sauce, the coriander, ginger, garlic, salt and pepper in medium bowl; mix well.

3. Spoon pork mixture into squid bodies, packing loosely and filling to 1 inch of top. Insert head sections into bodies, leaving tentacles hanging out; skewer with wooden picks to secure. Shape remaining pork mixture into 1-inch balls.

4. Combine broth, onions, remaining 2 tablespoons fish sauce and the sugar in large saucepan. Heat over medium heat to boiling.

5. Add squids and pork balls to soup; heat over medium heat until soup just comes to a boil. Reduce heat to low; skim foam. Simmer, uncovered, over medium-low heat until pork is cooked, about 10 minutes. Remove and discard onions. Ladle soup into bowls; stir in green onions. Serve immediately.

*Makes 6 servings*

# Fox Noodles

(Kitsune Udon)

3 quarts water
4 ounces udon (dried wheat noodles)
3 cups cold water
4 pieces (6×3×¼ inch each) abura-age (deep fried tofu) (about 2 ounces)
2 long onions or 8 green onions, white part only
5 cups Dashi (see page 48)
4½ tablespoons soy sauce
2½ tablespoons saké
1½ tablespoons sugar
3 tablespoons chopped green onions
Shichimi togarashi (seven-spice powder)

1. Heat 2 quarts of the water in large saucepan over high heat to boiling. Gradually add udon, stirring gently. When water returns to a boil, add 1 cup of the cold water; repeat 2 more times, using remaining cold water. When water returns to boiling, check for doneness; cook only until firm-tender. (Total cooking time will vary depending on thickness of noodles but should be 8 to 12 minutes.)

2. Drain noodles; transfer to large bowl. Fill bowl with cool water, stirring noodles with hands to rinse. Drain; repeat rinsing process until water remains clear. Drain noodles; cover with damp kitchen towel.

3. Cut abura-age crosswise into 1-inch-wide strips. Cut long onions diagonally into ½-inch-thick slices.

4. Heat Dashi in medium saucepan over medium heat to simmering. Add soy sauce, saké and sugar; heat to simmering. Add abura-age and long onions; simmer over medium heat, 3 minutes.

5. To reheat noodles, heat remaining 1 quart water in large saucepan over high heat to boiling. Add noodles; stir briefly. Drain immediately.

6. Divide noodles among 4 bowls. Ladle broth, abura-age and long onions over noodles. Serve immediately with chopped green onions and shichimi togarashi to taste.

*Makes 4 servings*

1          3          5          6

# Egg Drop Soup

(Kakitama-Jiru)

**3 ounces boneless skinless chicken**
**½ teaspoon plus pinch salt**
**1 teaspoon saké**
**1 piece (1 inch) carrot (about**
    **1¼ inches in diameter)**
**¾ cup water**
**2 large eggs**
**1 quart Dashi (see page 48)**
**1 teaspoon light soy sauce**

1. Cut chicken into ½×½×1½-inch-oblong pieces. Combine pinch salt, the saké and chicken in small bowl; reserve.

2. Cut carrot crosswise into ⅛-inch-thick slices; if desired, cut slices into decorative shapes using knife or vegetable cutter. Place water and ¼ teaspoon salt in saucepan. Heat to boiling over medium-high heat; add carrot slices. Cook 2 minutes; drain.

3. Mix eggs well with fork; do not beat.

4. Place Dashi in 3-quart saucepan; heat to boiling over medium-high heat. Add remaining ¼ teaspoon salt, the soy sauce and chicken. Reduce heat to medium; boil soup 2 minutes.

5. Slowly pour about ⅓ of egg mixture at a time into boiling soup, stirring constantly. Soup must return to boiling before each addition of egg. Turn off heat immediately after last egg "threads" form.

6. Place 2 carrot slices into each of 4 soup bowls. Ladle about 1 cup of soup over carrot slices in each bowl.

*Makes 4 servings*

# SALADS

# Chicken and Cucumber Salad

(Goi Ga Tom)

1 quart plus 3 tablespoons water
3 chicken thighs (about 14 ounces)
1 large carrot
2 medium cucumbers
1 teaspoon salt
2 tablespoons nuoc mam (fish sauce)
1½ tablespoons fresh lime juice
1½ tablespoons sugar
1 clove garlic, finely chopped
½ cup roasted unsalted peanuts
4 shelled deveined jumbo shrimp, cooked (about 3 ounces)
1 tablespoon chopped fresh coriander leaves
1 tablespoon chopped fresh mint leaves
1 tablespoon chopped fresh basil leaves
1 tablespoon chopped green onion, tops only
⅓ cup vegetable oil
8 prawn crackers

1. Heat 1 quart of the water in medium saucepan over high heat to boiling. Add chicken. Reduce heat to low; simmer, covered, until tender, about 25 minutes. Drain chicken; let stand until cool enough to handle.

2. Cut carrot into 2×⅛×⅛-inch strips. Cut cucumbers in half lengthwise; scoop out and discard seeds. Cut cucumbers crosswise into ¹⁄₁₆-inch slices.

3. Combine carrot and cucumbers in large bowl; sprinkle with salt. Toss to mix well; let stand 15 minutes.

4. Meanwhile, skin and debone chicken; cut into ¼-inch cubes.

5. For dressing, combine remaining 3 tablespoons water, the nuoc mam, lime juice, sugar and garlic in small bowl; stir until sugar is dissolved.

6. Chop peanuts; crush slightly in mortar with pestle or on board with rolling pin.

7. Squeeze carrot and cucumbers between hands to extract liquid; discard liquid.

8. Combine carrot and cucumbers with chicken and peanuts in medium bowl; drizzle with dressing. Toss to mix well; refrigerate, covered, 30 minutes to 2 hours.

9. Cut shrimp in half lengthwise, leaving attached at tails. Mix coriander, mint, basil and green onion in small bowl.

10. Just before serving, heat oil in wok over high heat until oil is very hot. Reduce heat to medium-low; fry prawn crackers, 2 or 3 at a time, just until they puff, 5 to 10 seconds. Drain on paper towels.

11. Transfer salad mixture to deep serving dish. Garnish with shrimp; top with mixed herbs. Serve with prawn crackers. *Makes 4 servings*

2                      7                      8                      10

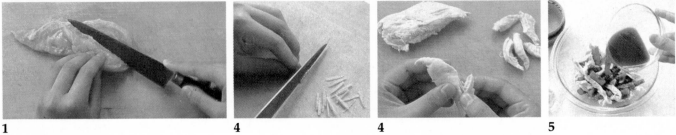

1      4      4      5

# Chicken-Asparagus Salad

(Tori Karashi-Ae)

4 ounces skinless boneless chicken
    breast
1 tablespoon plus 1 teaspoon saké
¾ teaspoon salt
3 cups water
6 medium stalks asparagus
1 piece (1 inch square) lemon rind
3 tablespoons soy sauce
½ teaspoon prepared Japanese
    mustard

1. Cut chicken horizontally into ½-inch-thick pieces. Place chicken in small saucepan; sprinkle with 1 teaspoon saké and ½ teaspoon salt. Let stand 10 minutes.

2. Add 1 cup water to chicken; heat to boiling over high heat. Reduce heat to low; simmer until chicken is cooked through, 2 to 3 minutes. Drain chicken, reserving 1 tablespoon of the cooking liquid. Cool completely.

3. Cut asparagus stalks into 1-inch lengths. Heat remaining 2 cups water and ¼ teaspoon salt to boiling in medium saucepan; add asparagus. Reduce heat to medium; cook until

asparagus is crisp-tender, 3 to 5 minutes. Drain asparagus; cool completely.

4. Cut lemon rind into ¹⁄₁₆-inch-wide strips; reserve. Tear chicken into ½×1-inch strips. Combine chicken and asparagus in medium bowl.

5. Place reserved cooking liquid, remaining 1 tablespoon saké, the soy sauce and mustard in small bowl; mix well. Pour mixture over chicken and asparagus; toss lightly to coat. Divide mixture evenly among 4 bowls, if desired. Sprinkle with lemon strips.

*Makes 4 servings*

# Red and White Salad

(Namasu)

⅓ cup rice vinegar
3 tablespoons sugar
3 tablespoons salt
1 kyuri (Japanese cucumber) (about 6 ounces)
12 ounces daikon (Japanese white radish), pared
1 large carrot
Cold water

1. To make vinegar dressing, combine vinegar, sugar and ¼ teaspoon of the salt in small saucepan. Heat over medium-low heat until sugar and salt are dissolved and mixture is steaming, about 3 minutes; do not boil. Remove from heat; let stand until cool.

2. Rub kyuri firmly with 1 tablespoon of the salt to smooth and cleanse skin; rinse well. Cut kyuri diagonally into ¹⁄₁₆-inch slices, discarding ends. Stack slices and cut lengthwise into ¹⁄₁₆-inch strips.

3. Cut daikon crosswise into 2-inch pieces. Cut each piece lengthwise into ¹⁄₁₆-inch slices, then cut each slice into ¹⁄₁₆-inch strips. Repeat procedure to cut carrot into ¹⁄₁₆-inch strips.

4. Combine kyuri, daikon and carrot strips in large bowl; sprinkle with remaining salt. Toss to mix; let stand 10 minutes.

5. Pour off liquid that has collected in bowl of vegetables. Fill bowl with cold water; stir and gently squeeze vegetables in water with hands. Pour off water and repeat rinsing procedure 2 more times.

6. Remove vegetables from water, a handful at a time, squeezing firmly to extract as much water as possible; discard water.

7. Combine vegetables and vinegar dressing in medium bowl; mix well. Let stand at room temperature, stirring occasionally, 1 hour. Salad can be refrigerated, covered, up to 3 days. Drain before serving.

*Makes 6 to 8 servings*

# Seaweed and Tuna with Soy Dressing

(Wakame Sujoyu-Ae)

⅓ ounce wakame (salted dried seaweed)
1½ quarts water
3 tablespoons rice vinegar
2 tablespoons soy sauce
1 teaspoon sugar
1½ teaspoons sesame oil
10 to 12 ounces canned water-packed tuna, drained
1½ teaspoons lemon juice
1 small thin cucumber, preferably unwaxed (3 to 4 ounces)
1 large tomato

1. Place wakame and 3 cups water in large bowl; let stand 20 minutes. Drain wakame. Heat remaining 3 cups water to simmering in 2-quart saucepan over medium-high heat. Add wakame; simmer 30 seconds. Rinse under cold running water; drain well.

2. Lay wakame out flat on work surface; cut away and discard any hard veins. Cut wakame strips into 1-inch lengths.

3. For dressing, mix vinegar, soy sauce, sugar and oil in small bowl; stir to dissolve sugar. Reserve.

4. Place tuna in medium bowl; break up with fork into bite-sized pieces. Sprinkle with lemon juice.

5. Cut cucumber crosswise into 1/16-inch-thick slices. Cut tomato into ¾-inch cubes.

6. Add wakame, cucumber and tomato to tuna; add dressing and toss lightly until thoroughly mixed. Transfer to medium serving bowl or to 4 individual bowls, dividing evenly.

*Makes 4 servings*

4

5

5

6

# Clam Salad with Miso Dressing

(Asari Nuta)

2 tablespoons rice vinegar
1 tablespoon plus ½ teaspoon saké
1 tablespoon white miso (bean paste)
2 teaspoons sugar
½ teaspoon light soy sauce
4 ounces shucked very small fresh clams
3 cups water
6 green onions
¼ teaspoon salt

1. For dressing, mix vinegar, 1 tablespoon saké, the miso, sugar and soy sauce in small bowl; stir to dissolve sugar. Reserve.

2. Place clams, 1 cup water and remaining ½ teaspoon saké in 2-quart saucepan; heat to boiling over medium-high heat. Reduce heat to medium; boil gently just until cooked through, about 1 minute. Drain; cool completely.

3. Cut green onions into 1-inch lengths. Heat remaining 2 cups water and the salt to boiling in 2-quart saucepan over medium-high heat. Add white parts of onions and thicker green parts to pan; boil 1 minute. Add green tops of onions; boil 1 minute longer. Drain; cool completely.

4. Combine clams and onions in medium bowl; add dressing. Toss lightly until thoroughly mixed. Transfer to medium serving bowl or to 4 individual bowls, dividing evenly.

*Makes 4 servings*

2

3

4

# Mixed Vegetables with Peanut Sauce

(Jaganan)

8 ounces fresh green beans, trimmed
8 ounces cabbage
4½ quarts water
6 ounces fresh mung bean sprouts, rinsed and trimmed
1 medium cucumber, pared
2 medium potatoes, pared and boiled
2 or 3 hard-cooked eggs, shelled
6 ounces fried pressed tofu
⅓ cup vegetable oil
8 to 12 prawn crackers

Peanut Sauce
3 long thin hot fresh red chili peppers, seeded
2 cloves garlic
1 shallot
1 teaspoon shrimp paste
3 tablespoons vegetable oil
1 cup roasted unsalted peanuts
1 cup water
2 tablespoons white vinegar
1½ tablespoons sugar
½ teaspoon salt

1. Cut green beans crosswise into 1½-inch pieces. Cut cabbage in ½-inch-wide shreds.

2. Heat 6 cups of the water in medium saucepan over high heat to boiling. Add bean sprouts; cook 10 seconds. Drain immediately; rinse briefly under cold running water to stop the cooking. Drain well. Repeat procedure with green beans and 6 cups boiling water, cooking beans until crisp-tender, about 4 minutes. Repeat procedure with cabbage and 6 cups boiling water, cooking cabbage 2 minutes.

3. Score cucumber lengthwise with tines of fork; cut crosswise into ¼-inch slices. Cut potatoes and eggs crosswise into ¼-inch slices. Cut tofu in half lengthwise, then cut crosswise into ¼-inch slices.

4. Arrange cucumber, potatoes, tofu, bean sprouts, green beans, cabbage and eggs attractively on large shallow serving platter. Refrigerate, covered, until about 20 minutes before serving.

5. Heat oil in wok over high heat until oil is very hot. Reduce heat to medium-low; fry prawn crackers, 2 or 3 at a time, just until they puff, 5 to 10 seconds. Drain on paper towels.

6. Make Peanut Sauce just before serving. Chop chilies, garlic and shallot; place in food processor or blender with shrimp paste. Process, adding up to 1 tablespoon of the oil, until mixture is ground into a fine paste. Grind peanuts, in batches, in electric spice mill to a fine powder. Gradually add ground peanuts to chili paste and process just until evenly mixed.

7. Heat remaining oil in medium skillet over medium heat until hot. Add chili-peanut mixture; stir-fry 3 minutes. Stir in water; reduce heat to low. Cook, stirring constantly, until sauce thickens, 3 to 4 minutes. Stir in vinegar, sugar and salt; remove from heat.

8. Serve arranged vegetable platter with prawn crackers. Pass hot Peanut Sauce, spooning sauce over individual servings. *Makes 4 to 6 servings*

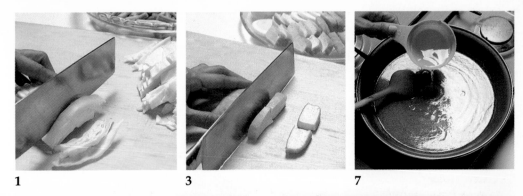

**1**  **3**  **7**

# Pickled Cabbage

(Kimchi)

1 large head Chinese cabbage
   (napa or bok choy)
   (about 3 pounds)
1½ cups coarse (Kosher) salt
6 cups water
1 small bunch green onions,
   3 to 4 ounces
8 ounces daikon (Japanese white
   radish), pared
1 small head garlic,
   10 to 12 cloves, chopped
1 piece (1×¾ inches) pared fresh
   ginger root, chopped
⅓ cup Korean anchovy sauce or
   fish sauce
3 to 4 tablespoons Korean red
   pepper powder
1½ tablespoons sugar

1. Cut cabbage lengthwise into wedges; rinse and drain well. Starting with bottom leaf and keeping wedges intact, sprinkle each leaf with some of the salt. Place wedges in large bowl.

2. Mix remaining salt with water; pour over cabbage. Top with plate and 2-pound weight, such as canned goods. Let stand, at room temperature, until cabbage is wilted, at least 2 hours.

3. Meanwhile, cut onions crosswise into 2½-inch lengths, then cut each piece into ⅛-inch strips. Cut daikon diagonally into ¹⁄₁₆-inch slices, then cut each slice into ¹⁄₁₆-inch strips.

4. Pound garlic and ginger together in mortar with pestle to fine paste; combine with fish sauce, red pepper and sugar in medium bowl. Stir in onions and daikon.

5. Drain cabbage; rinse thoroughly under cold running water, allowing water to run over both sides of each leaf to remove as much salt as possible. Drain cabbage again, squeezing each wedge firmly between hands to extract as much liquid as possible.

6. Starting with bottom leaf and keeping wedges intact, spread some of the daikon mixture over each leaf. Leaving bottom leaf of each wedge extended, fold wedge crosswise in half; pull bottom leaf out to side and wrap around cabbage to make neat compact bundle.

7. Place cabbage bundles (kimchi) in large bowl or jar; press down firmly to release any trapped air. Pour any remaining daikon mixture over cabbage. Let stand, covered, at room temperature, 12 hours. Refrigerate, covered, at least 48 hours before serving.

8. To serve, unwrap and unfold kimchi wedge; cut crosswise into 1½-inch pieces and arrange on serving plate.
*Makes 16 to 24 servings*
*(about 2 quarts)*

Note: Kimchi will keep in refrigerator up to 2 weeks.

# Chinese Mixed Pickles

**Pickling Liquid**
  3 cups sugar
  3 cups white vinegar
1½ cups water
1½ teaspoons salt

**Pickles**
  3 large carrots
  1 large white Chinese radish
      (about 1 pound)
  1 large cucumber
  4 stalks celery
  8 green onions
  4 ounces fresh ginger root
  1 large red bell pepper
  1 large green bell pepper

**For Pickling Liquid**
1. Combine all ingredients in 3-quart saucepan. Cook and stir over medium heat until liquid boils. Remove from heat. Cool.

**For Pickles**
2. Wash all vegetables. Pare carrots and radish. Cut cucumber lengthwise into quarters and remove seeds. Cut carrots, radish and cucumber into matchstick-thin strips about 2 inches long. Cut celery into ½-inch diagonal slices. Cut onions into ¼-inch diagonal slices. Pare ginger root and cut into thin slices. Remove seeds from peppers and cut peppers into ½-inch cubes.

3. Fill a Dutch oven half full of water. Cover and heat over high heat until water boils. Uncover and add all vegetables. Remove from heat immediately. Let vegetables stand uncovered 2 minutes.

4. Drain vegetables in large colander. Spread vegetables out on clean towels and allow to dry 2 or 3 hours.

5. Pack vegetables firmly into clean jars with lids. Pour Pickling Liquid into jars until vegetables are completely covered. Cover jars tightly. Store in refrigerator at least 1 week before using.      *Makes 1½ to 2 quarts*

# MEATS

## Mu Shu Pork

16 Mandarin Pancakes (recipe
    follows)
5 teaspoons soy sauce
5 teaspoons dry sherry
4 teaspoons cornstarch
8 ounces boneless lean pork, cut
    into matchstick pieces
3 dried black Chinese mushrooms
2 dried wood ears
    Hot water
7 teaspoons vegetable oil, divided
2 large eggs, lightly beaten
1 tablespoon water
½ teaspoon sugar
1 teaspoon sesame oil
1 teaspoon minced fresh ginger
    root
½ cup sliced bamboo shoots
    (½ of 8-ounce can), cut into
    matchstick pieces
1 small carrot, shredded
½ cup chicken broth
2 cups fresh mung bean sprouts
    (about 4 ounces), rinsed and
    trimmed
2 green onions, cut into 1½-inch
    slivers
½ cup hoisin sauce

1. Prepare Mandarin Pancakes.

2. For marinade, combine 2 teaspoons
of the soy sauce, 2 teaspoons of the
sherry and 1 teaspoon of the cornstarch in large bowl. Add pork and stir
to coat. Let marinate at room temperature 30 minutes.

3. Place dried mushrooms and wood
ears in small bowl and cover with hot
water. Let soak in hot water 30 minutes. Drain. Trim and discard mushroom stems; squeeze out excess water.
Cut mushroom caps into thin slices.

Pinch out hard knobs from center of
wood ears and discard; cut wood ears
into thin strips.

4. Heat ½ teaspoon of the vegetable oil
in small nonstick skillet over medium-
high heat until hot. Add half of the
eggs and tilt skillet to cover bottom.
Cook just until egg is set. Loosen
edges, turn omelet over and cook
other side 5 seconds. Remove from
skillet and repeat procedure with another ½ teaspoon of the vegetable oil
and remaining egg. When omelets are
cool, cut in half. Stack halves and cut
crosswise into ⅛-inch strips.

5. For sauce, combine remaining 3
teaspoons soy sauce, 3 teaspoons
cornstarch and 3 teaspoons sherry in
small bowl. Add the water, sugar and
sesame oil; mix well.

6. Heat remaining 6 teaspoons vegetable oil in wok or large skillet over high
heat until hot. Add ginger and stir
once. Add pork; stir-fry until meat is
no longer pink, about 2 minutes. Add
mushrooms, wood ears, bamboo
shoots, carrot and chicken broth; stir-
fry 2 minutes. Add bean sprouts and
onions; stir-fry 1 minute.

7. Quickly stir cornstarch mixture;
pour into wok. Cook, stirring constantly, until sauce bubbles and thickens. Stir in omelet strips.

8. To serve, spread about 2 teaspoons
hoisin sauce on each pancake. Spoon
about 3 tablespoons pork mixture
down center. Fold in bottom and roll
up. *Makes 8 servings*

3

4

### Mandarin Pancakes
2 cups all-purpose flour
¾ cup boiling water
2 tablespoons sesame oil

1. Place flour in bowl and make a well
in center. Pour in boiling water; stir
with wooden spoon until dough looks
like lumpy meal. Press into a ball.
Knead dough on lightly floured work
surface until smooth and satiny, about
5 minutes. Cover with clean towel and
let stand 30 minutes.

2. Roll dough into 10-inch-long log.
Cut into 10 equal pieces; keep covered.

3. Cut one piece of dough in half. Roll
each half into a ball; flatten slightly.
Roll each piece on lightly floured work
surface into a 3-inch circle. Brush top

of each with sesame oil. Stack dough circles together, oil-side in. Roll the pair together into a 6- to 7-inch circle. Repeat for remaining pieces of dough. (Keep uncooked pancakes covered while rolling out remaining dough.)

4. Heat nonstick skillet over medium-low heat. Cook pancakes, 1 pair at a time, turning every 30 seconds, until cakes are flecked with brown and feel dry, 2 to 3 minutes. (Be careful not to overcook; cakes become brittle.)

5. Remove from pan and separate into 2 pancakes while still hot. Stack between layers of waxed paper on plate and keep covered while cooking remaining pancakes. Serve at once, refrigerate or freeze in resealable plastic bag. To reheat, wrap pancakes in clean towel (thaw completely, if using frozen). Steam over simmering water 5 minutes. Fold pancakes into quarters and arrange in serving basket.

*Makes 20 pancakes*

# Sweet and Sour Pork

2½ pounds lean pork chops
¼ cup soy sauce
1½ tablespoons dry sherry
2 teaspoons sugar
1 large egg yolk
1 large yellow onion
8 green onions
1 red or green bell pepper
4 ounces fresh mushrooms
2 stalks celery
1 medium cucumber
10 tablespoons cornstarch
3 cups vegetable oil
1 cup water
1 can (20 ounces) pineapple
   chunks in syrup
3 tablespoons vegetable oil
¼ cup white vinegar
3 tablespoons tomato sauce

1. Trim chops, discarding fat and bones. Cut pork into 1-inch pieces. Mix soy sauce, sherry, sugar and egg yolk in large glass bowl. Mix in pork. Cover and let stand 1 hour, stirring occasionally.

2. Cut yellow onion into thin slices. Cut green onions into thin diagonal slices. Remove seeds from pepper and

chop coarsely. Clean mushrooms and cut into halves or quarters. Cut celery into ½-inch-diagonal slices. Cut cucumber lengthwise into quarters and remove seeds. Cut cucumber into ¼-inch-wide pieces.

3. Drain pork, reserving soy sauce mixture. Coat pork with 8 tablespoons of the cornstarch. Heat 3 cups oil in pan over high heat until it reaches 375°F. Cook ½ of the pork in oil until brown, about 5 minutes. Drain on paper towels. Cook and drain remaining pork.

4. Combine water and remaining 2 tablespoons cornstarch. Drain pineapple, reserving syrup. Heat 3 tablespoons oil in wok over high heat. Add all the prepared vegetables to oil. Stir-fry 3 minutes. Add the syrup, reserved soy sauce mixture, vinegar and tomato sauce to vegetables. Add cornstarch mixture to vegetables. Cook and stir until sauce boils and thickens. Add pork and pineapple. Cook and stir until hot throughout.

*Makes 6 servings*

# Szechuan Pork Shreds with Green Beans

1 pound boneless pork loin,
      trimmed
1½ ounces pared fresh ginger root
2 tablespoons soy sauce
4 teaspoons sugar
1 tablespoon rice wine
2 teaspoons cornstarch
1 teaspoon sesame oil
1 pound tender young green beans
      or Chinese long beans
2 tablespoons cold water
1 teaspoon water chestnut flour
1 tablespoon hot bean paste
1¼ cups peanut oil
1 clove garlic, sliced

1. For easier slicing, freeze pork until firm but not frozen, 30 to 40 minutes. Cut pork across the grain into ⅛-inch-thick slices; then cut slices into 2×¼-inch shreds.

2. Grate ginger. Mix ginger, 1 tablespoon of the soy sauce, 2 teaspoons of the sugar, the rice wine, cornstarch and sesame oil in medium bowl; stir in pork shreds. Marinate at room temperature 15 to 30 minutes.

3. Cut green beans crosswise into 2-inch pieces; pat very dry with paper towels. Mix water and water chestnut flour in small bowl; stir in remaining 1 tablespoon soy sauce, remaining 2 teaspoons sugar and the hot bean paste.

4. Heat peanut oil in wok over high heat until oil reaches 375°F. Adjust heat to maintain temperature. Place strainer in deep heatproof bowl.

5. Gradually add beans to oil while gently stirring; fry until beans begin to wrinkle and turn brown, about 10 seconds after all the beans have been added. Immediately drain beans in strainer.

6. Return 3 tablespoons of the hot peanut oil to wok. Heat wok over high heat until oil is hot, about 30 seconds. Reduce heat to medium; add garlic and fry until brown, about 10 seconds. Remove and discard garlic.

7. Increase heat to high. Stir-fry pork, ⅓ at a time, until brown, 1½ to 2 minutes after all pork is added. Quickly stir bean paste mixture and add to center of wok. Stir-fry until sauce thickens, 15 to 30 seconds. Stir in beans; stir-fry just until heated and coated with sauce, about 15 seconds. Serve immediately.

*Makes 3 to 4 servings*

# Ginger Pork Saute

(Butaniku Shoga-Yaki)

**1 pound boneless lean pork loin or tenderloin**
**4 ounces Chinese cabbage (napa or bok choy)**
**3 tablespoons soy sauce**
**1 tablespoon fresh ginger juice**
**1 tablespoon saké**
**1 teaspoon sugar**
**2 tablespoons vegetable oil**

1. For easier slicing, freeze meat until firm but not frozen, 30 to 40 minutes.

2. Cut pork crosswise into ⅛-inch-thick slices. Cut slices into 2-inch pieces.

3. Remove hard center sections from cabbage leaves, if necessary. Cut cabbage into 1-inch squares.

4. Mix soy sauce, ginger juice, saké and sugar in small bowl; stir until sugar dissolves.

5. Heat 1 tablespoon oil in 10-inch skillet over high heat. Add pork; saute, stirring constantly, until pork is half cooked, about 3 minutes. Remove pork from pan; reserve.

6. Add remaining 1 tablespoon oil to skillet. Add cabbage; saute, stirring constantly, until almost tender, 1 to minutes. Return pork to skillet; add soy-sauce mixture. Cook, stirring occasionally, until pork is cooked through, 2 to 3 minutes. Serve immediately. *Makes 4 servings*

# Minced Pork in Lettuce Leaves

¼ cup roasted unsalted peanuts
1 ounce small shallots
1 fresh red chili pepper, seeded
3 tablespoons fresh lemon juice
2 tablespoons fish sauce
1½ teaspoons sugar
1½ pounds lean ground pork
¼ cup coarsely chopped fresh
   coriander leaves
3 tablespoons sliced green onion,
   tops only
1½ tablespoons minced pared fresh
   ginger root
12 iceberg lettuce leaves
6 whole green onions

1. Coarsely grind peanuts in mortar with pestle. Cut shallots lengthwise into very thin slices. Cut chili lengthwise into very thin slivers.

2. Combine lemon juice, fish sauce and sugar in small bowl; stir until sugar is dissolved.

3. Heat medium skillet over medium heat until hot, about 1 minute. Add pork; cook and stir, breaking pork into small pieces, until it is cooked, but not brown, 8 to 10 minutes. Remove from heat. Tilt skillet; spoon off and discard all but 2 tablespoons fat.

4. Add peanuts, shallots, coriander, green onion tops and ginger to pork; mix well. Drizzle with lemon juice mixture; mix well. Transfer to serving dish; top with chili pepper slivers.

5. To serve, spoon pork mixture into lettuce leaves; serve with whole green onions. *Makes 6 servings*

# Pork and Chicken Adobo

1 pound boneless pork loin
1¼ pounds chicken thighs
    (about 4 large)
½ cup white vinegar
3 tablespoons soy sauce
4 cloves garlic, crushed through
    press
1 teaspoon salt
¼ to ½ teaspoon ground black
    pepper
¾ cup water
2 tablespoons vegetable oil

1. Cut pork across the grain into ¾-inch slices, then cut slices into 2×1-inch pieces. Combine with chicken in large bowl.

2. Mix vinegar, soy sauce, garlic, salt and pepper in small bowl; pour over pork and chicken. Marinate at room temperature, stirring occasionally, 1 hour.

3. Transfer pork-chicken mixture to medium nonaluminum saucepan; stir in water. Heat over medium heat to boiling. Reduce heat to low; simmer, covered, until pork and chicken are tender, about 30 minutes.

4. Remove pork and chicken with slotted spoon, draining well. Transfer to plate. Cook vinegar mixture over high heat until reduced to coating consistency, about 15 minutes.

5. While sauce is reducing, heat oil in medium skillet over medium heat; add pork. Cook, turning frequently, until brown on all sides, about 3 minutes. Remove to plate. Add chicken to skillet; cook, turning once, until brown, about 2 minutes. Arrange chicken and pork on serving plate; keep warm.

6. Strain sauce through fine sieve; skim and discard fat. Pour sauce over chicken and pork.

*Makes 4 servings*

# Twice-Cooked Pork with Bean Sauce

7 green onions, white part only
    Ice water
2 cups water
1 pound boneless pork loin blade
    roast
8 ounces Chinese cabbage (napa or
    bok choy)
1 large green bell pepper, seeded
1½ tablespoons hoisin sauce
1 tablespoon black bean sauce
    with chili
2 tablespoons rice wine
1 tablespoon soy sauce
1 teaspoon sugar
3 tablespoons peanut oil
2 teaspoons minced pared fresh
    ginger root
1 teaspoon minced garlic

1. For garnish, use 3 of the green onions. With thin-bladed knife, make ¾-inch-long cuts through one end of each onion at ⅛-inch intervals. Repeat cuts at other end of each onion, leaving at least 1 inch at center of onion uncut. Place onions in medium bowl of ice water; refrigerate. Onions will open into flowers.

2. Heat water in small saucepan over high heat to boiling; add pork. Reduce heat to medium-low; cook, covered, turning meat over once, 35 minutes. Remove pork; plunge into large bowl of ice water. Let chill 20 minutes.

3. Cut cabbage leaves lengthwise into 1-inch-wide slices, then cut crosswise into 2-inch pieces. Cut green pepper lengthwise into 1-inch strips, then cut strips in half crosswise. Cut each half diagonally into 2 triangles. Cut remaining 4 green onions diagonally into 1-inch lengths.

4. Remove pork from water; pat dry with paper towels. Cut pork across the grain into ⅛-inch slices, then cut slices into 2×¾-inch pieces. Mix hoisin sauce and black bean sauce with chili in small bowl. Mix rice wine, soy sauce and sugar in second small bowl.

5. Heat 1½ tablespoons oil in wok over high heat until hot, about 30 seconds. Stir-fry green pepper, cabbage and green onion pieces 1 minute. Transfer to plate.

6. Heat remaining 1½ tablespoons oil in wok until hot. Reduce heat to medium; stir-fry ginger and garlic 5 seconds. Increase heat to high; add pork and stir-fry until brown, 2 to 3 minutes. Reduce heat to medium and add hoisin sauce mixture to wok; stir-fry until sauce is fragrant and pork is evenly coated, about 30 seconds.

7. Return vegetables to wok; stir-fry 30 seconds. Increase heat to high; add rice wine mixture and stir-fry until sauce is reduced to coating consistency, about 30 seconds. Transfer mixture to serving dish. Drain green onion flowers well; cut crosswise into halves, forming 2 flowers each. Place on top of pork; serve immediately.

*Makes 3 to 4 servings*

# Pork and Vegetable Platter

(Yudebuta)

**1¼ pounds boneless lean pork loin or leg roast**
**2 quarts water**
**1 small leek**
**4 slices (⅛ inch thick) pared fresh ginger root**
**4 medium potatoes**
**2 large carrots**
**4 ounces green beans, trimmed**
**Mustard Sauce (recipe follows)**
**Sesame Seed Sauce (see page 144)**

1. Tie pork at ¾-inch intervals with kitchen twine. Place pork in 3- or 4-quart saucepan; add 1½ quarts water (use more water, if necessary, to cover pork).

2. Cut leek crosswise into 1-inch lengths. Add leek and ginger to pork. Heat to boiling over high heat; reduce heat to medium. Boil gently, turning pork occasionally, 30 minutes.

3. Meanwhile, pare potatoes; cut into halves or quarters. Place potatoes and remaining 2 cups water in medium bowl. Soak 5 minutes; drain. Cut carrots crosswise into 1½-inch lengths; cut lengthwise into halves or quarters. Cut beans in half crosswise.

4. Prepare Mustard Sauce and Sesame Seed Sauce.

5. Add potatoes and carrots to pork; add boiling water, if necessary, to cover pork and vegetables. Boil gently until pork is cooked through, 15 to 20 minutes longer. (To test pork for doneness, pierce center of thickest part with knife; juice should run clear.) Add beans to pork; cook until beans are crisp-tender, 3 to 5 minutes.

6. Drain pork and vegetables; discard leek and ginger. Remove twine from pork. Cut pork into ¼-inch-thick slices; arrange on serving platter with vegetables. Serve with Mustard Sauce and Sesame Seed Sauce for dipping.

*Makes 4 serving*

## Mustard Sauce

**¼ cup soy sauce**
**1 tablespoon sugar**
**¼ teaspoon grated pared fresh ginger root**
**1 to 2 teaspoons prepared Japanese mustard**

Mix soy sauce, sugar and ginger in small bowl; stir to dissolve sugar. Add mustard; stir until smooth.

*Makes about 5 tablespoon*

# Deep-Fried Pork Cutlets

(Tonkatsu)

8 ounces cabbage
  Ice water
1 pound pork tenderloin
¾ teaspoon salt
½ teaspoon sansho powder
    (Japanese fragrant pepper)
1 large egg
1 teaspoon water
⅓ cup all-purpose flour
1 cup panko (Japanese dry bread
    crumbs)
3 cups vegetable oil
4 tomato wedges
4 parsley sprigs
½ cup tonkatsu sosu (spicy sauce)
4 teaspoons Oriental hot mustard

1. Cut cabbage into fine shreds; place in large bowl of ice water. Let stand while proceeding with recipe.

2. Cut pork crosswise into ¾-inch slices. Pound slices with flat side of meat mallet, flattening to ⅜-inch thickness. Sprinkle both sides of pork with salt and sansho.

3. Beat egg with 1 teaspoon water in shallow bowl. Dip pork in flour to coat; shake off excess. Dip in egg, then in panko; press pieces between palms to help coating adhere.

4. Heat oil in wok over high heat until oil reaches 350°F. Adjust heat to maintain temperature. Fry 2 or 3 pieces of pork at a time until golden brown and cooked through but not dry, about 2½ minutes per side. Drain on paper-towel-lined wire rack.

5. Drain cabbage thoroughly. Arrange pork and cabbage on serving plates; garnish with tomato and parsley. Serve with tonkatsu sosu and mustard for dipping. *Makes 4 servings*

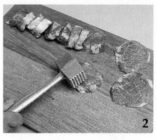

# Caramel Ribs

1½ pounds pork spareribs
½ pound pork belly (fresh bacon), skinned*
2 tablespoons vegetable oil
¼ cup finely chopped green onion
1½ teaspoons minced pared fresh ginger root
1 clove garlic, minced
3½ tablespoons soy sauce
2 teaspoons black mushroom soy sauce**
2½ teaspoons salt
1 cup plus 1 tablespoon sugar
⅛ teaspoon ground black pepper
2 small thin cucumbers, preferably seedless
1 tablespoon minced fresh parsley

1. Cut spareribs into individual ribs; chop each rib crosswise with cleaver into 1½-inch pieces. (Or ask your butcher to cut the ribs.) Cut pork belly into 1½×1-inch pieces. Rinse meat well to remove any bone fragments; drain well.

2. The success of this recipe depends on using a properly sized and shaped pan. Use a deep, narrow, heavy 2½-quart saucepan, 4 to 5 inches deep and 6 to 7 inches in diameter. This will allow the meat to fit snugly so that the juices will cover it during cooking and not evaporate too quickly and burn. Heat saucepan over high heat 1 minute.

3. Add oil; heat 30 seconds. Reduce heat to medium; add onion, ginger and garlic. Cook and stir 30 seconds.

4. Increase heat to high. Add meat, 1 handful at a time, stirring well after each addition so that meat is seared. Continue cooking, after all meat is added, until it is no longer pink and just begins to brown, about 3 minutes.

5. Reduce heat to medium; add soy sauce and black mushroom soy sauce. Add salt, then add 1 cup of the sugar and the pepper; stir to mix well.

6. Increase heat to high; heat to boiling. Sugar will melt and juices will bubble up around meat. Adjust heat so that level of juices remains bubbling just over surface of meat but does not overflow pan, about medium. Stir to mix well.

7. Cook meat, uncovered, 15 minutes. DO NOT STIR. Cool small spoonful of sauce slightly and taste; if too salty, stir in remaining 1 tablespoon sugar. Continue cooking, stirring occasionally and watching so that sauce does not burn (reduce heat if necessary), until meat is cooked and sauce is thickened to glaze consistency, about 15 minutes longer.

8. While meat is cooking, cut out 4 evenly spaced shallow wedges lengthwise from each cucumber. Cut cucumbers crosswise into thin slices.

9. Transfer meat with slotted spoon to serving dish; spoon sauce over meat. Arrange cucumber slices in ring around meat; sprinkle with parsley.

*Makes 3 to 4 servings*

*Pork belly is available in Asian and Mexican grocery stores. It can be omitted if desired; use 2 pounds spareribs and increase oil to 3 tablespoons.

**Black mushroom soy sauce has a richer, slightly sweeter flavor than regular soy sauce. If necessary, regular soy sauce can be substituted.

# Mongolian Lamb

**Sesame Sauce**
  1 tablespoon sesame seeds
  ¼ cup soy sauce
  1 tablespoon dry sherry
  1 tablespoon red wine vinegar
1½ teaspoons sugar
  1 clove garlic, minced
  1 green onion, minced
  ½ teaspoon sesame oil

**Lamb**
  16 ounces boneless lean lamb (leg or shoulder)
  2 small leeks, cut into 2-inch slivers
  4 green onions, cut into 2-inch slivers
  2 medium carrots, shredded
  1 medium zucchini, shredded
  1 red bell pepper, cut into matchstick pieces
  1 green bell pepper, cut into matchstick pieces
  ½ small head napa cabbage, thinly sliced
  1 cup fresh mung bean sprouts, rinsed and trimmed
  4 tablespoons vegetable oil
  4 slices pared fresh ginger root
  Chili oil (optional)

1. For sauce, toast sesame seeds in small dry skillet over medium heat, stirring constantly, until golden, about 2 minutes. Transfer to plate; let cool. Pound seeds in mortar with pestle; transfer to small serving bowl. Add soy sauce, sherry, vinegar, sugar, the minced garlic and onion and the sesame oil; mix well.

2. Slice lamb across the grain into ¼×2-inch strips.

3. Arrange meat and vegetables on large platter. Have Sesame Sauce, vegetable oil, ginger and chili oil near cooking area.

4. At serving time, heat electric griddle or wok to 350°F. Cook one serving at a time. For each serving, heat 1 tablespoon of the vegetable oil; add 1 slice of the ginger and cook 30 seconds; discard. Add ½ cup of the meat strips; stir-fry until lightly browned, about 1 minute. Add 2 cups assorted vegetables; stir-fry 1 minute. Drizzle with 2 tablespoons of the Sesame Sauce; stir-fry 30 seconds. Season with a few drops of the chili oil, if desired. Repeat procedure for next 3 servings with remaining ingredients.

*Makes 4 servings*

1

2

3

# Lamb Curry

Turmeric Potatoes (recipe
   follows)
¼ cup vegetable oil
2½ pounds boneless lamb shoulder
   or leg, cut into 1½-inch cubes
3 tablespoons Ghee (recipe
   follows)
3 medium onions, minced
2 tablespoons minced pared fresh
   ginger root
3 cloves garlic, minced
2 tablespoons ground coriander
2 teaspoons ground turmeric
2 teaspoons ground cumin
1 teaspoon ground red pepper
3 cups boiling water
2 large tomatoes, peeled and
   pureed in food processor or
   blender
2 teaspoons salt
½ teaspoon sugar
3 tablespoons finely chopped fresh
   coriander
   Slivered fresh red chili pepper
   Fresh coriander sprig

1. Prepare Turmeric Potatoes through step 1.

2. Heat oil in Dutch oven over high heat until hot. Add as much lamb as will fit in single layer without crowding; cook, turning frequently, until brown on all sides, about 8 minutes. Remove lamb to plate; repeat procedure until all lamb has been browned.

3. Add Ghee to pan and heat until hot. Add onions; cook, stirring constantly, over medium-high heat until light brown, about 10 minutes. Add ginger and garlic; cook and stir 30 seconds. Add ground coriander, turmeric, cumin and red pepper; cook and stir just until fragrant, about 10 seconds.

4. Add lamb; stir in boiling water, tomatoes, salt and sugar. Heat to boiling; reduce heat to maintain simmer. Simmer, uncovered, until lamb is very tender, 1½ to 2 hours.*

5. About 20 minutes before serving, finish preparing Turmeric Potatoes. Just before serving, stir chopped coriander into simmering curry; simmer 1 minute. Transfer curry to one side of serving platter; arrange Turmeric Potatoes next to curry. Garnish with slivered chili and coriander sprig.

*Makes 6 to 8 servings*

*Flavor of curry will be improved if made ahead to this point and allowed to stand at least 1 hour (or curry can be refrigerated overnight). Reheat to simmering just before serving.

## Turmeric Potatoes

3 cups water
1½ pounds small boiling potatoes,
   unpared, scrubbed
¾ teaspoon salt
½ teaspoon ground turmeric
⅛ teaspoon ground red pepper
3 tablespoons vegetable oil

1. Heat water in small saucepan over high heat to boiling. Add potatoes. Reduce heat to medium-low; cook, covered, just until firm-tender when pierced with knife, about 20 minutes. Drain potatoes; rinse under cold running water. Let cool completely, at least 2 hours.

2. Peel potatoes; cut into 1-inch wedge-shaped pieces. Mix salt, turmeric and red pepper in small bowl; sprinkle over potatoes in large bowl and toss to coat.

3. Heat oil in large skillet over medium-high heat until hot; add potatoes. Cook, stirring gently and turning frequently, until potatoes are golden brown and crusty, 7 to 10 minutes.

*Makes 6 to 8 servings*

## Ghee (Indian Clarified Butter)

½ pound unsalted butter, diced

1. Melt butter in heavy, medium saucepan over low heat. Increase heat to medium; butter will begin to sizzle as water evaporates. Let cook until sizzling stops, indicating that all water has evaporated, 10 to 20 minutes.

2. After water has evaporated, begin stirring constantly and watching carefully. Continue cooking until milk solids that have settled to bottom turn golden; immediately remove from heat. Strain butter through several layers of fine cheesecloth into clean jar; cool completely. Store Ghee, tightly covered, in refrigerator several weeks or in freezer several months.

*Makes about ¾ cup*

Note: Ghee is also available in many Indian grocery stores.

# Lamb Sate

2 pounds boneless leg of lamb
2 tablespoons kecap manis (sweet
    dark soy sauce)
2 cloves garlic, minced

**Soy Dip**
2 tablespoons kecap manis
1 medium tomato, finely chopped
⅓ cup thinly sliced shallots
1 or 2 hot fresh red chili peppers,
    seeded and minced
¼ cup soy sauce
1 tablespoon fresh lime juice

**Peanut Dip**
⅓ cup Fried Onion Flakes
    (see page 35)
1 or 2 hot fresh red chili peppers,
    seeded and chopped
1 clove garlic, chopped
1 teaspoon sugar
¼ teaspoon salt
½ cup crunchy peanut butter
½ cup boiling water
¼ teaspoon kecap manis (optional)

2 tablespoons vegetable oil
Pressed Rice Cake (see page 34),
    sliced (optional)

1. Place 32 bamboo or wooden 8-inch skewers in warm water. Soak for 20 minutes.

2. Trim and discard all fat from lamb. Cut lamb across the grain into ⅓-inch slices, then cut slices into 1-inch squares. Mix lamb, kecap manis and minced garlic in medium bowl. Marinate at room temperature, stirring occasionally, 1 hour.

3. For Soy Dip, combine kecap manis, tomato, shallots and chilies in small bowl; stir in soy sauce and lime juice, mixing well.

4. For Peanut Dip, grind Fried Onion Flakes, chilies, garlic, sugar and salt to fine paste in mortar with pestle or in blender; transfer to small bowl. Add peanut butter; gradually add water, stirring until smooth. Transfer to small serving bowl. Drizzle kecap manis over surface of dip in fine line; run tip of knife through surface several times to create swirled pattern.

5. Drain skewers; thread 4 pieces of lamb on each skewer. Grill over charcoal or broil, about 6 inches from heat, turning and brushing occasionally with oil, until cooked, 4 to 6 minutes. Serve with dips and sliced Pressed Rice Cake. *Makes 6 to 8 servings*

# Curried Minced Meat with Peas

(Keema Mattar)

2 large onions
2 medium potatoes
    (about 6 ounces each), pared
1 medium tomato
2 long thin fresh green chili
    peppers, seeded
½ cup vegetable oil
1¼ pounds lean ground beef or
    lamb
2 tablespoons tomato paste
1 tablespoon minced garlic
1 tablespoon paprika
1 tablespoon ground cumin
1½ teaspoons ground turmeric
1½ teaspoons grated pared fresh
    ginger root
1½ teaspoons salt
1 teaspoon ground cardamom
1 piece (3 inches) cinnamon stick
½ to ¾ cup water
¾ cup fresh or frozen peas
½ cup chopped fresh coriander
    leaves
Chapatis*

1. Cut onions, potatoes and tomato into ⅜-inch square pieces. Cut chilies lengthwise into ¼-inch strips.

2. Cook and stir onions in oil in Dutch oven over medium heat until golden, about 15 minutes. Add potatoes; cook and stir 5 minutes.

3. Add meat; cook and stir over medium heat, breaking meat into small pieces, until it is no longer pink, about 10 minutes.

4. Add tomato paste, garlic, paprika, cumin, turmeric, ginger, salt, cardamom and cinnamon to pan; saute over medium heat 30 seconds. Quickly stir in ½ cup water; simmer, covered, over low heat 5 minutes.

5. Add diced tomato, chilies, peas and coriander; mix well. Simmer, covered, over low heat 10 minutes. Stir in remaining water if mixture becomes too thick. Serve with chapatis.

*Makes 6 servings*

*Chapati, an Indian flat bread made from whole wheat flour, is available in Indian grocery stores. Curried Minced Meat would also be good served with flour tortillas or pita bread.

# Meat and Vegetable Casserole

## (Shabu-Shabu)

1½ pounds well-marbled boneless
    beef sirloin
10 leaves Chinese cabbage (napa or
    bok choy)
8 fresh shiitake mushrooms or
    12 white mushrooms
3 long onions or 1 large bunch
    green onions, white part only
1½ quarts water
3½ ounces dried shirataki filaments
    Ponzu Sauce (recipe follows)
4 lemon wedges
3 cups chicken broth
¼ cup grated pared daikon
    (Japanese white radish)
¼ cup thinly sliced green onion
    tops

1. For easier slicing, freeze beef until firm but not frozen, 30 to 40 minutes.

2. Meanwhile, cut cabbage leaves into 2-inch squares. Remove and discard mushroom stems; make shallow V-shaped cuts in star pattern on each mushroom cap. Cut long onions diagonally into ¼-inch slices, or cut green onions into ½-inch slices.

3. Heat 1 quart of the water in medium saucepan over high heat to boiling. Add shirataki; boil 2 minutes. Drain and rinse under cold running water to stop the cooking; drain well. Cut roughly into 3- or 4-inch pieces.

4. Cut beef across the grain into 1/16-inch-thick slices, then cut slices into 3- or 4-inch-long pieces. Arrange meat slices folded and overlapping on platter.

5. Make Ponzu Sauce. Divide among 4 small bowls.

6. Arrange cabbage, mushrooms, long onions, shirataki, Ponzu Sauce and lemon wedges on large tray.*

7. Place chicken broth and remaining 2 cups water in medium saucepan. Heat over medium-high heat to boiling. Transfer to appropriate cooking vessel.** Adjust heat to maintain temperature.

8. To cook, each person, using chopsticks or fondue fork, swishes pieces of meat or vegetables, 1 at a time, back and forth in simmering broth mixture until cooked to desired doneness, 15 to 30 seconds for meat and 1 to 2 minutes for vegetables. Dip cooked food into Ponzu Sauce.

9. When the meat and vegetables have been eaten, add shirataki to remaining broth mixture; cook just until heated. Ladle into soup bowls and serve with remaining Ponzu Sauce, daikon and green onion tops.

*Makes 4 servings*

*Other foods suitable for Shabu-Shabu include spinach leaves, blanched sliced carrots and tofu cubes.

**Appropriate vessels for table-cooking include Mongolian hot pot; cast-iron pot; flameproof casserole; chafing dish; fondue pot; or deep-sided electric skillet or electric wok. If vessel is not electric, a portable adjustable heat source is needed.

3

4

## Ponzu Sauce

    ½ cup soy sauce
    ¼ cup fresh lemon juice
    2 tablespoons rice vinegar

Combine all ingredients. Reserve at room temperature. (Refrigerate, covered, any leftover sauce.)

# Beef and Vegetable Rolls

(Gyuniku Yasai-Maki)

2 pieces (1×6 inches each) carrot
2 pieces (1×6 inches each) burdock
  root
4¼ cups water
1 teaspoon vinegar
4 teaspoons vegetable oil
1½ tablespoons plus 1 teaspoon
  sugar
¼ teaspoon salt
16 to 24 green beans, trimmed
3 tablespoons soy sauce
1 tablespoon mirin
8 slices (⅛×2×9 inches each) lean
  beef
1½ to 2½ tablespoons cornstarch
1 tablespoon saké
4 sprigs watercress (optional)

1. Cut each carrot piece in half lengthwise; cut each half lengthwise into 4 equal strips. Scrape burdock root with back of knife to remove all skin; cut as for carrot. Place burdock root immediately into small bowl with 1½ cups water and the vinegar; soak 5 minutes. Rinse and drain.

2. Heat 1 teaspoon vegetable oil in 8-inch skillet over medium-high heat. Add carrot and burdock strips; saute, stirring constantly, 2 minutes. Add ½ cup water and 1 teaspoon sugar; cook just until vegetables are tender, about 5 minutes longer. Drain carrot and burdock.

3. Heat 2 cups water and the salt to boiling in 2-quart saucepan over medium-high heat. Add green beans; cook, covered, just until tender, about 3 minutes. Cool under cold running water; drain.

4. Mix remaining ¼ cup water and 1½ tablespoons sugar, the soy sauce and mirin in small bowl. Stir until sugar dissolves; reserve.

5. Lay beef slices flat on work surface; sift cornstarch lightly onto one side of each slice. Place 2 strips each of carrot and burdock and 2 or 3 green beans crosswise at slight angle on end of slice

of beef. Roll beef diagonally, jelly-roll fashion, around vegetables; secure with wooden pick. Repeat with remaining beef and vegetables. Lightly dust outside of each roll with cornstarch.

6. Heat remaining 1 tablespoon vegetable oil in 12-inch skillet over high heat. Add beef rolls; saute, turning occasionally, until brown on all sides, to 4 minutes. Add saké; cook 30 seconds. Add reserved soy-sauce mixture; heat to boiling. Reduce heat to low; simmer rolls, turning constantly, until well coated with slightly thickened sauce, 3 to 5 minutes. Remove from heat.

7. Carefully cut each roll in half crosswise. Transfer to serving platter; garnish with watercress. Pass any remaining sauce. *Makes 4 servings*

# Sesame Beef

(Bulgogi)

**2 pounds boneless beef sirloin or
  top round steak**
**¼ cup sesame seeds**
**1 small bunch green onions
  (about 3 ounces)**
**⅔ cup soy sauce**
**⅓ cup water**
**⅓ cup sugar**
**2½ tablespoons sesame oil**
**2 to 3 cloves garlic, minced**
**⅜ teaspoon ground black pepper
  Large parsley sprig**

1. For easier slicing, freeze beef until firm but not frozen, 30 to 40 minutes.

2. Meanwhile, toast sesame seeds in small dry skillet over medium heat, stirring constantly, until golden, about 5 minutes; transfer to plate and let cool. Pound seeds in mortar with pestle until partially ground (about half the seeds should be powdery).

3. Cut beef across the grain into ⅛-inch-thick slices. Cut onions crosswise into 2½-inch pieces; then cut each piece into fine shreds.

4. Combine soy sauce, water, sugar, sesame seeds, sesame oil, garlic and pepper in medium bowl, stirring until sugar is dissolved. Stir in onions.

5. Dip beef slices, 1 at a time, into soy sauce mixture, coating both sides. Arrange slices overlapping in large bowl, spreading several pieces of onion between each layer. Marinate, covered, at room temperature 1 hour.

6. Heat large nonstick or well-seasoned skillet over high heat until hot. Add as many beef slices to skillet as will fit in single layer without crowding. Cook, turning occasionally, until liquid is absorbed and meat be-

gins to brown, 1½ to 3 minutes. Remove to heated serving platter; keep warm. Immediately add more meat to skillet to prevent drippings from burning. Repeat procedure until all meat is cooked; discard any remaining marinade. Garnish with parsley; serve immediately.

*Makes 6 to 8 servings*

Note: Sesame Beef can be cooked over charcoal or in a broiler. Place meat about 5 inches from heat; watch carefully so that meat does not overcook or burn.

# Braised Anise Beef

1 piece (2×1 inch) fresh ginger
   root, scrubbed
2 cloves garlic
2 pounds boneless beef chuck
   roast
2 star anise
1 piece (1 inch) cinnamon stick
1½ tablespoons sugar
⅓ cup soy sauce
1 cup water
2 tablespoons rice wine
1½ teaspoons sesame oil (optional)
2¼ teaspoons cornstarch mixed with
   1½ tablespoons cold water
   Fluted Cucumber Cup*
   (optional)

1. Lightly pound ginger and garlic with flat side of cleaver to smash slightly.

2. Place beef in large saucepan or flameproof casserole. Top beef with ginger, garlic, star anise and cinnamon; sprinkle with sugar. Pour soy sauce over beef; add 1 cup water.

3. Heat over high heat to boiling. Reduce heat to low; simmer, covered, turning beef over every 30 minutes, until beef is fork-tender, about 2 hours. Remove from heat; stir in rice wine and sesame oil.

4. To serve beef hot, remove from pan; let stand 10 minutes. Cut crosswise into thin slices; arrange on platter and garnish with Fluted Cucumber Cup.

5. Skim fat from cooking liquid. Remove and discard ginger and garlic. To thicken, add cornstarch-water mixture to 1½ cups of the cooking liquid. Simmer over medium heat, stirring constantly, until thickened, about 3 minutes.

6. To serve beef cold, transfer beef and cooking liquid to medium bowl, discard ginger and garlic; let cool completely. Refrigerate, covered, until cold. Remove and discard fat from sauce. Cut beef crosswise into thin slices; serve with cold sauce.

*Makes 4 to 6 servings*

*To make Fluted Cucumber Cup, cut 2-inch-long piece of cucumber. Insert thin paring knife between skin and flesh; cut around cucumber to detach and remove skin in one piece. Cut 1 inch-long cuts at ⅓-inch intervals around one end of cucumber skin. Trim tip of each cut piece into a point. Cut cucumber into thin slices and stack inside of skin.

# Pan-Broiled Garlic Steak

(Gyuniku Nimiku-Yaki)

4 boneless beef top loin steaks,
    ½-inch thick (about 6 ounces
    each)
1 clove garlic, minced
¼ cup soy sauce
1½ tablespoons mirin
6 ounces daikon (white Japanese
    radish), pared
1 piece (3 inches long) large carrot
    (about 2 ounces)
1 cube (1 inch) pared fresh ginger
    root
¼ cup rice vinegar
1½ tablespoons sugar
1 tablespoon vegetable oil
¼ cup thinly sliced green onions,
    tops only

1. Make several short, shallow cuts against the grain on each steak. Place in large, shallow noncorrosive pan or glass dish. Mix garlic, soy sauce and mirin in small bowl. Pour over steaks; let stand 20 minutes, turning occasionally. Drain.

2. Cut daikon and carrot lengthwise into 1½-inch lengths; cut lengthwise into ⅛16-inch-thick slices. Stack slices and cut lengthwise into ⅛16-inch-wide strips. Cut ginger into ⅛16-inch-thick slices; stack slices and cut into ⅛16-inch-wide strips.

3. Stir vinegar and sugar in small bowl until sugar dissolves. Add daikon, carrot and ginger; let stand 5 minutes. Drain; squeeze lightly to remove excess moisture.

4. Heat vegetable oil in 12-inch skillet over medium-high heat. Add beef; saute until brown, about 3 minutes. Turn, saute until beef is cooked to desired doneness, 3 to 5 minutes.

5. Place beef on individual serving plates; sprinkle each serving with 1 tablespoon green onion. Serve with vegetable mixture.

*Makes 4 servings*

1

2

2

# Rare Beef Cubes

(Gyuniku Sashimi)

1 pound beef tenderloin,
    about 2-inches thick
7 ounces daikon (white Japanese
    radish)
2 green onions, tops only
1 small lemon
2 teaspoons vegetable oil
1 quart ice water
1 tablespoon soy sauce
1 teaspoon mirin

1. Trim fat from beef. Cutting against the grain, cut beef in half.

2. Grate daikon; drain any excess liquid (but do not squeeze). Cut green onions into ⅛-inch thick slices. Cut lemon in half crosswise. Cut four ⅛-inch-thick slices from one half of lemon. Squeeze juice from remaining half; reserve.

3. Brush beef lightly on all sides with 1 teaspoon oil. Heat remaining 1 teaspoon oil in medium skillet over high heat. Add beef; saute just until brown, turning to brown all sides,

about 2 minutes. Immediately transfe[r] beef into ice water; let stand 2 minutes Drain beef; pat dry with paper towels Cut into 1-inch cubes.

4. Mix soy sauce and mirin in a cup Divide beef cubes among 4 individua[l] serving bowls. Add lemon slice and grated daikon; top with green onion. Sprinkle with soy-sauce mixture and lemon juice. Pass additional soy sauce if desired. *Makes 4 serving[s]*

1                    2                    3

# Soy-Seasoned Beef and Potatoes

(Nikujaga)

12 ounces boneless beef sirloin
1 pound potatoes
    (about 4 medium)
1 quart water
2 medium onions
1 cube (1 inch) pared fresh ginger
    root
5 teaspoons vegetable oil
3 tablespoons saké
2 tablespoons sugar
3 tablespoons soy sauce

1. For easier slicing, freeze meat until firm but not frozen, 30 to 40 minutes.

2. Cut beef across the grain into ¹⁄₁₆- to ⅛-inch-thick slices. Cut each slice into

1½-inch lengths. Pare potatoes and cut into quarters; cut quarters crosswise into 1-inch pieces. Place potatoes in 3 cups water in large bowl; soak 5 minutes. Drain.

3. Cut onions in half lengthwise; cut halves crosswise into ⅛-inch-thick slices. Cut ginger into ¹⁄₁₆-inch-thick slices; stack slices and cut into ¹⁄₁₆-inch-wide strips. Reserve ginger.

4. Heat 2 teaspoons oil in heavy, 3-quart saucepan over medium-high heat. Add beef; saute, stirring occasionally, just until brown, about 2 minutes. Remove from pan; reserve.

5. Add remaining 3 teaspoons oil t[o] pan; heat over medium-high heat unti[l] hot. Add onions and potatoes; saute stirring constantly to coat well with oil about 2 minutes.

6. Add remaining 1 cup water, th[e] saké and sugar to pan; heat to boiling Reduce heat to medium; boil gently 1[0] minutes. Add soy sauce and beef t[o] pan; boil gently until potatoes ar[e] tender, 10 to 15 minutes. Serve imme diately, with cooking liquid, garnishe[d] with ginger strips.

*Makes 4 serving[s]*

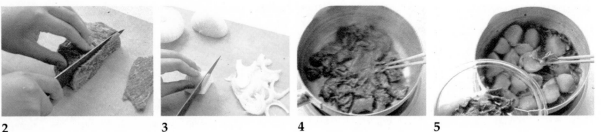

2                    3                    4                    5

# Spiced Coconut Beef

(Rendang)

2½ pounds boneless beef rump or
    round roast
5 stalks fresh lemon grass
1 large onion, chopped
6 to 8 cloves garlic, chopped
1 piece (2×1×1 inches) pared fresh
    ginger root
1 tablespoon ground turmeric
2 tablespoons water
1½ cups Thin Coconut Milk
½ cup shredded fresh turmeric
    leaves (optional)
1 piece (1 inch) fresh galingal or
    1½ teaspoons ground laos
    powder
1 to 3 teaspoons hot red chili
    powder
2 dried citrus leaves
1 cup Rich Coconut Milk
    (see page 173)
1½ teaspoons sugar
¾ teaspoon salt
    Fresh Red Chili Flower*
    (optional)

1. Cut beef across the grain into ¼-inch slices.

2. Trim root end of lemon grass. Cut off tapering upper green leaf portion, leaving about 5-inch-long bulbous stalk. Peel off tough outer layers of bulbous stalk. Discard all trimmings. Pound 4 of the remaining tender parts of stalks lightly with flat side of cleaver to smash slightly; reserve. Mince remaining stalk.

3. Place minced lemon grass, onion, garlic, ginger and ground turmeric in food processor or blender. Process until finely ground, scraping down sides of container as needed. With motor running, add water in slow stream; continue processing until pureed to smooth paste.

4. Heat Thin Coconut Milk in large saucepan over medium heat to boiling. Add beef; mix well. Heat to simmering. Add ground paste, reserved lemon grass stalks, turmeric leaves, galingal, chili powder and cit-

rus leaves; mix well. Adjust heat to maintain strong simmer, about medium-low. Cook, uncovered, stirring occasionally, until beef is almost tender, about 1 hour.

5. Stir in Rich Coconut Milk; increase heat to medium-high. Cook, uncovered, stirring frequently, until almost all liquid has evaporated and beef is coated with very thick sauce, about 1 hour; watch carefully during last 20 minutes of cooking to prevent burning.

6. Remove and discard lemon grass stalks, galingal and citrus leaves; stir in sugar and salt. Transfer to serving dish; garnish with Chili Flower.

*Makes 6 to 8 servings*

*To make Fresh Red Chili Flower, cut long thin fresh red chili pepper lengthwise, starting ½ inch from stem end, into 6 or 8 petals; discard seeds. Place chili in small bowl with ice water to cover. Refrigerate 1 hour.

# Miso Marinated Beef Slices

(Gyuniku Miso-Zuke)

3 tablespoons miso (bean paste)
1½ tablespoons sugar
1½ tablespoons saké
1 tablespoon soy sauce
1 pound boneless beef sirloin slices, about ¼ inch thick
2 cups water
¼ teaspoon salt
4 stalks asparagus
2 medium leeks
1 tablespoon vegetable oil

1. Place miso, sugar, saké and soy sauce in shallow bowl or pie plate; stir to mix well. Add beef; coat slices thoroughly. Let stand 20 minutes; scrape off miso mixture from beef.

2. Heat water and salt to boiling in 2-quart saucepan over medium-high heat; add asparagus. Boil just until asparagus begins to soften, about 2 minutes. Drain well. Cut leeks in half crosswise.

3. Heat oil in 12-inch skillet over medium heat. Add beef; saute, turning occasionally, until brown and cooked through, 2 to 3 minutes. Remove from skillet to warm serving plate.

4. Add asparagus and leeks to skillet; saute over medium heat, turning occasionally, until tender, 1 to 1½ minutes. Remove from skillet; cut into 2-inch lengths. Serve beef and vegetables immediately. *Makes 4 servings*

Note: Beef and vegetables may be grilled, if desired. Grill beef over medium heat, turning once, 2 to 4 minutes. Brush asparagus with 1 teaspoon oil (do not boil). Grill asparagus and leeks over medium heat, turning occasionally, just until tender. Sprinkle asparagus with salt after grilling.

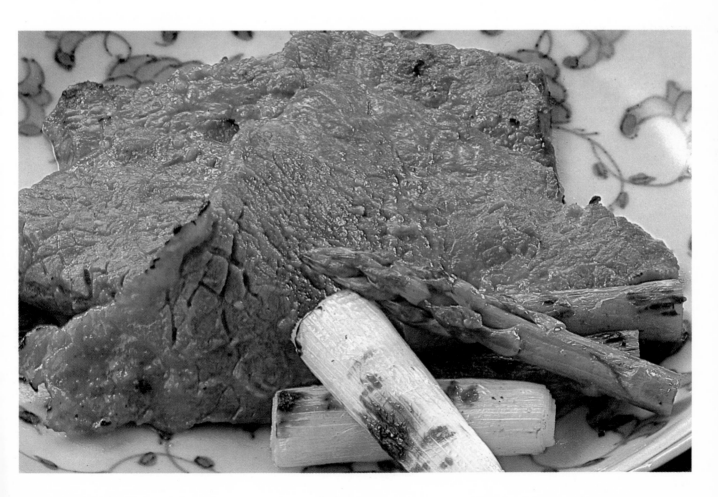

# Beef and Vegetable Saute

(Sukiyaki)

1 pound boneless beef sirloin or
    tenderloin
1 quart plus ½ cup water
8 ounces shirataki filaments
10 to 12 ounces tofu
8 to 10 medium fresh black
    Chinese mushrooms
2 medium leeks
4 ounces fresh spinach, washed,
    well drained
4 large eggs*
½ cup soy sauce
¼ cup saké
¼ cup mirin
3 tablespoons sugar
2 ounces beef suet, cut into
    2 or 3 pieces

1. For easier slicing, freeze meat until firm but not frozen, 30 to 40 minutes.

2. Cut beef into ¹⁄₁₆-inch-thick slices. Cut slices into 3- to 4-inch lengths.

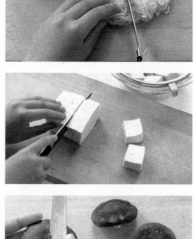

3

3. Heat 1 quart water to boiling in 2-quart saucepan over high heat. Add shirataki; boil 2 minutes. Drain well; cut into 4-inch lengths. Cut tofu into 1- to 1½-inch cubes; drain.

3

4. Remove and discard stems from mushrooms; make shallow, V-shaped cuts in criss-cross design on cap of each mushroom, if desired. Cut leeks diagonally into ½-inch-thick slices. Cut spinach leaves in half crosswise.

4

5. Arrange beef, shirataki, tofu, mushrooms, leeks and spinach on large platter. Break 1 egg into each of 4 small serving bowls.

6. Mix remaining ½ cup water, the soy sauce, saké, mirin and sugar in medium bowl or pitcher; stir to dissolve sugar. Reserve sauce.

4

7. At the table, heat 10- to 12-inch skillet over medium-high heat.** Add beef suet; heat until partially melted and pan is evenly coated. Add several beef slices; cook until just beginning to brown, about 1 minute. Add about ½ of the sauce and about ⅓ of the tofu, shirataki, mushrooms, leeks and spinach, as well as more beef slices. Cook, turning ingredients to coat with sauce, until foods reach desired doneness. As each kind of food is cooked, diners are served or serve themselves from the skillet. Each person mixes the egg and uses as dipping sauce for hot food. Add food and sauce to skillet as needed until all ingredients are cooked. *Makes 4 servings*

*Use only clean, uncracked Grade A eggs.

**For cooking at the table, use electric skillet, or use chafing dish or heavy skillet with portable heat source, such as a hot plate. If unavailable, cook on top of range and serve immediately. Food must be served hot so that light coating of egg actually "cooks" onto food when dipped.

# Beef with Celery and Mushrooms

1 pound boneless top sirloin or
    round steak
2½ tablespoons soy sauce
1½ tablespoons rice wine
1½ teaspoons sugar
 ¼ teaspoon ground black pepper
1 tablespoon cornstarch
5 tablespoons peanut oil
3 large ribs celery
2 tablespoons water
1 can (6 ounces) button
    mushrooms, well drained
2 tablespoons minced pared fresh
    ginger root
2 cloves garlic, minced

1. For easier slicing, freeze beef until firm but not frozen, 30 to 40 minutes.

2. Cut beef across the grain into ⅛-inch-thick slices; then cut slices into 2×1½-inch pieces.

3. Combine beef, 2 tablespoons of the soy sauce, 1 tablespoon of the rice wine, the sugar and pepper in medium bowl. Sprinkle with cornstarch; mix well. Stir in 1 tablespoon of the oil. Marinate at room temperature 30 minutes.

4. Cut celery diagonally into ½-inch slices. Mix water and the remaining ½ tablespoon soy sauce and ½ tablespoon rice wine in small bowl.

5. Heat 2 tablespoons of the oil in wok over high heat until hot, about 30 seconds. Stir-fry celery 1½ minutes. Remove to plate.

6. Drain beef, reserving marinade mixture.

7. Add remaining 2 tablespoons oil to wok; heat until hot. Reduce heat to medium; stir-fry mushrooms, ginger and garlic 30 seconds. Increase heat to high; stir-fry beef, adding ¼ at a time, until cooked, about 1 minute after all beef is added.

8. Return celery to wok; stir-fry until heated, about 30 seconds. Stir in marinade mixture; cook and stir until beef and vegetables are coated with sauce, about 30 seconds. Serve immediately.
*Makes 3 to 4 servings*

# Beef with Green Peppers

1 pound boneless top sirloin or
    rump steak
3 tablespoons soy sauce
3 tablespoons rice wine
1 teaspoon sugar
1 tablespoon cornstarch
6 tablespoons peanut oil
2 large green bell peppers, seeded
2 tablespoons water
1½ tablespoons oyster sauce
3 tablespoons minced green onion,
    white part only
2 teaspoons minced pared fresh
    ginger root

1. For easier slicing, freeze beef until firm but not frozen, 30 to 40 minutes.

2. Cut beef across the grain into ¼-inch slices. Combine beef, 2 tablespoons of the soy sauce, 2 tablespoons of the rice wine and the sugar in medium bowl. Sprinkle with cornstarch; mix well. Stir in 1 tablespoon oil. Marinate at room temperature 30 minutes.

2

2

3. Cut peppers lengthwise into 1-inch strips. Mix water, oyster sauce and the remaining 1 tablespoon of soy sauce and 1 tablespoon of rice wine in small bowl.

4. Heat 2 tablespoons of the oil in wok over high heat until hot, 30 seconds. Stir-fry green peppers 45 seconds. Remove to plate.

5. Heat 2 tablespoons of the oil in wok over high heat until hot. Reduce heat to low; stir-fry onion and ginger 10 seconds. Increase heat to high; stir-fry beef, adding ¼ at a time, until cooked, about 2 minutes after all beef is added.

6. Return green peppers to wok; stir-fry until heated, about 15 seconds. Stir in oyster sauce mixture; stir-fry until beef and peppers are coated with sauce, about 30 seconds. Drizzle with remaining 1 tablespoon oil; stir 3 to 4 times. Serve immediately.

*Makes 3 to 4 servings*

3

# POULTRY

## Tandoori Chicken

4 chicken legs, thighs and
  drumsticks attached
  (about 2¼ pounds)*
1 tablespoon lemon juice
1 teaspoon yellow food coloring
½ teaspoon red food coloring
1½ tablespoons ground coriander
1 tablespoon paprika
1 tablespoon ground cumin
2 teaspoons salt
1¼ cups plain yogurt
1 tablespoon grated pared fresh
  ginger root
1 teaspoon garlic, crushed through
  press
¼ cup melted Ghee (see page 74) or
  vegetable oil
  Lemon wedges

1. Cut skin of chicken leg lengthwise with scissors. Remove and discard skin and excess fat.

2. Mix lemon juice and yellow and red food coloring in cup. Brush chicken with mixture to coat.

3. Mix coriander, paprika, cumin and salt in cup. Sprinkle mixture over chicken in shallow glass bowl or casserole, turning chicken and spreading spices to evenly coat.

4. Mix yogurt, ginger and garlic in small bowl. Pour yogurt mixture over chicken, turning pieces to coat. Marinate, covered, in refrigerator, turning pieces occasionally, 4 to 6 hours. Let chicken stand in marinade, covered, at room temperature 1 hour before cooking.

5. Heat oven to 500°F. Remove chicken from bowl, shaking off as much marinade as possible. Place chicken in single layer in greased shallow baking pan; brush chicken with 2 tablespoons Ghee.

6. Bake chicken 12 minutes. Turn pieces over; brush with remaining 2 tablespoons Ghee. Continue baking until chicken is cooked through and tender, about 13 minutes longer. Serve immediately with lemon wedges.

*Makes 4 servings*

*Tandoori Chicken can be made with chicken breasts in place of legs; reduce cooking time in Step 6 to about 10 minutes per side.

1

2

4

# Honey-Roast Chicken

1½ teaspoons Szechuan peppercorns
2 tablespoons soy sauce
1 teaspoon sesame oil
1 whole broiler-fryer chicken
   (3 to 3½ pounds)
1 tablespoon minced green onion,
   white part only
1 teaspoon minced pared fresh
   ginger root
1 clove garlic, minced
1 tablespoon honey
3 tablespoons coarse (Kosher) salt
½ teaspoon five-spice powder
   Water
1 large tomato (optional)

1. Roast peppercorns in small, heavy dry skillet over very low heat, shaking pan frequently, until pepper is fragrant and begins to smoke slightly, about 5 minutes. Let cool; crush until finely ground in mortar with pestle.

2. Mix soy sauce, sesame oil and half of the pepper in small bowl. Place chicken in large bowl. Brush soy sauce mixture over outside of chicken. Pour remaining mixture over chicken.

3. Mix onion, ginger and garlic in small bowl; rub well in cavity of chicken. Brush skin with honey. Marinate at room temperature, turning occasionally, 1 hour.

4. Roast salt in small, heavy dry skillet over medium-low heat, stirring occasionally, until salt begins to color, 5 to 8 minutes; transfer to small bowl. Cool slightly; stir in remaining pepper and the five-spice powder.

5. Heat oven to 400°F. Drain chicken, reserving marinade. Place chicken, breast side down, on rack in roasting pan. Roast chicken 15 minutes. Turn chicken onto one side; baste with marinade and continue roasting 15 minutes. Turn chicken onto second side; baste, then roast 15 minutes. Turn chicken breast side up; baste. Continue roasting until chicken is tender and brown and meat thermometer inserted into thickest part of thigh registers 180°F, 15 to 20 minutes longer. Add 1 cup water to pan as needed during roasting to prevent drippings from burning.

6. Remove chicken; let stand 10 minutes. Meanwhile, prepare the tomato garnish by using a small, sharp knife to cut the tomato into halves crosswise with V-shaped incisions. Cut wings and legs from chicken. Separate drumstick from thigh at joint. Separate back from breast portion; cut back crosswise into 4 pieces. Cut breast in half lengthwise; cut each half crosswise in halves.

7. Arrange chicken pieces on platter; garnish with tomato halves. Serve immediately with roasted spiced salt for dipping.
*Makes 4 servings*

3       4       7

# Skewered Grilled Chicken

(Yakitori)

4 long onions or 1 bunch green
    onions, white part only
½ cup soy sauce
2 tablespoons saké
1½ tablespoons mirin
2 teaspoons minced pared fresh
    ginger root
¼ teaspoon minced garlic
1 tablespoon vegetable oil
1 pound boneless skinless chicken
    breasts, cut into 1¼-inch
    pieces
¼ pound chicken livers (optional)
1 medium green bell pepper,
    seeded (optional)
2 tablespoons sugar

1. Place 12 bamboo or wooden 8-inch skewers in warm water.

2. Mince enough long onion to measure 3 tablespoons. Combine minced onion, soy sauce, saké, mirin, ginger and garlic in medium bowl; whisk in oil.

3. Add chicken to soy mixture; mix well. Marinate at room temperature, stirring occasionally, 30 minutes.

4. Meanwhile, cut remaining long onions crosswise into 1-inch pieces. Cut chicken livers in half. Cut green pepper into 1-inch pieces.

5. Drain chicken, reserving marinade. Transfer marinade to small saucepan; add sugar. Heat over high heat to boiling. Reduce heat to medium-low; simmer, uncovered, until slightly thickened, about 6 minutes. Reserve.

6. Drain skewers. Alternately thread chicken and onion on 8 skewers. Alternately thread chicken livers and green peppers on remaining 4 skewers.

7. Grill skewers over charcoal or broil, 4 inches from heat, turning once, 1 minute. Brush with marinade; continue grilling, brushing with marinade and turning every 30 seconds, until chicken is cooked, about 2 minutes. Serve immediately.

*Makes 4 main-dish servings*

Note: To serve as an appetizer, use 24 six-inch skewers. Divide food evenly among skewers. Makes 8 appetizer servings.

# Chicken and Vegetable Casserole

(Mizutaki)

2 pounds chicken pieces
2 quarts boiling water
1 piece (4 inches square) dried
     kelp (konbu)
2 tablespoons rice
3 quarts water
1 tablespoon saké
1 teaspoon salt
½ teaspoon sugar
4 leaves Chinese cabbage (napa or
     bok choy)
8 medium fresh black Chinese
     mushrooms
10 ounces tofu
2 leeks
1 large carrot, 1 to 1½ inches in
     diameter
8 ounces shirataki filaments
     Ponzu Sauce (see page 78)
5 to 6 tablespoons grated pared
     daikon, drained
     Pinch cayenne pepper
2 to 3 tablespoons thinly sliced
     green onion
     Lime or lemon wedges
     Seven-spice powder or shansho
     powder
2 cups cooked udon noodles
     (optional)

1. Using heavy knife or cleaver, cut chicken into 1½-inch pieces. Place in sieve or colander; pour 2 quarts boiling water slowly over chicken to rinse thoroughly.

2. Wipe kelp gently with damp cloth to remove any sand (but not the white powder) that may adhere to surface. Using scissors, cut kelp crosswise into 4 equal strips. Place rice in center of 4-inch square of cheesecloth; secure with string to form "rice bag."

3. Place chicken, kelp, 2 quarts water, the rice, saké, salt and sugar in large kettle; heat to boiling over medium-high heat. Remove and discard kelp just **before** water boils. Reduce heat to medium; simmer, skimming foam occasionally, until chicken is tender, about 30 minutes. Remove and discard rice. Remove chicken pieces and place in table-cooking utensil.* Strain cooking broth; add to chicken.

4. While chicken is simmering, cut cabbage leaves into 2-inch squares. Remove and discard stems from mushrooms; if desired, make shallow, V-shaped cuts in crisscross design on cap of each mushroom. Cut tofu into 1-inch cubes; drain. Cut leeks diagonally into ½-inch-thick slices.

5. Cut carrot crosswise into ¼-inch-thick slices; if desired, cut slices into decorative shapes using knife or vegetable cutter. Heat remaining 1 quart water to boiling in 2-quart saucepan over high heat. Place carrot slices in sieve and lower into boiling water; cook 1 minute. Rinse under cold running water; drain. Add shirataki to boiling water; cook 2 minutes. Drain well; cut into 4-inch lengths.

6. Prepare Ponzu Sauce. Mix daikon with cayenne pepper in small bowl. Arrange cabbage, mushrooms, tofu, leeks, carrot and shirataki on platter.**

7. At the table, heat chicken and broth to boiling over medium-high heat; add about ¼ each of the vegetables, shirataki and tofu to pot. As food is added to pot, adjust heat to maintain strong simmer. As each kind of food is cooked (2 to 4 minutes), diners are served or serve themselves from the cooking pot. Add remaining vegetables, shirataki and tofu, about ¼ at a time, as needed.

8. For each person, place ¼ cup Ponzu Sauce in individual small bowls. As food is served, dip pieces into sauce mixed with choice of daikon, green onion, lime and/or seven-spice powder. Pass remaining Ponzu Sauce as needed.

9. If desired, after chicken and vegetables are served, add cooked udon noodles to broth; simmer 3 minutes. Ladle into individual bowls; serve.

*Makes 4 servings*

*Appropriate utensils for table-cooking include Mongolian hot pot; cast-iron pot; earthenware pot or casserole; flameproof (not oven-proof) ceramic casserole; deep-sided electric skillet; chafing dish; or fondue pot. If utensil is not electric, a portable heat source, with adjustable heat, is needed. If necessary use 2 utensils; divide broth and cook in both simultaneously. If unavailable, cook on top of range and serve immediately.

**Recipe can be prepared up to this point several hours in advance. Cool chicken and broth to room temperature; refrigerate. Wrap ingredients on platter in plastic wrap; refrigerate. Allow all to come to room temperature before cooking.

1                    1                    3                    5

# Wine-Simmered Chicken and Daikon

(Toriniku Daikon Budoshu-Ni)

1 pound boneless skinless chicken
    breasts or thighs
8 ounces daikon, pared*
1¾ cups water
1½ tablespoons soy sauce
1½ teaspoons sugar
1 tablespoon mirin
    Pinch salt
3 tablespoons dry red wine*

1. Cut chicken breasts into 1½-inch-square pieces.

2. Cut daikon into 1-inch irregularly shaped pieces.

3. Heat water to boiling in 2-quart saucepan over medium heat; add chicken and daikon. Boil gently 10 minutes.

4. Add soy sauce, sugar, mirin and salt to saucepan; boil gently until chicken is tender, 10 to 15 minutes longer. Add red wine to chicken; cook 1 to 2 minutes. Serve immediately with cooking liquid.  *Makes 4 servings*

*If daikon is very hot, increase amount of red wine to ¼ cup.

1            2            3

# Chicken Meatballs

(Toriniku Dango)

4 ounces green beans, trimmed
1 pound ground chicken
1 tablespoon plus 2 teaspoons
    sugar
¼ cup soy sauce
1 medium egg
1½ tablespoons cornstarch
3 cups Dashi (see page 48)
1½ tablespoons saké
1½ tablespoons mirin

1. Cut beans crosswise in half or thirds. Reserve.

2. Mix chicken, 2 teaspoons sugar, 1 tablespoon soy sauce and the egg in medium mixing bowl. Sprinkle with cornstarch; stir to mix well.

3. Mix Dashi, saké, mirin and remaining 3 tablespoons soy sauce and 1 tablespoon sugar in 3-quart saucepan; heat to boiling over medium-high heat.

4. Form chicken mixture into 1-inch balls. Add chicken balls, 1 at a time, to boiling broth; boil until chicken is cooked, 5 to 6 minutes. Remove balls from broth with slotted spoon.

5. Add beans to broth; cook until beans are crisp-tender, 2 to 3 minutes. Remove beans from broth. Serve chicken balls with beans; top with hot cooking broth, if desired.

*Makes 4 servings*

1            2            4

# Chicken and Chinese Sausage Rice

1¼ pounds chicken thighs
¼ pound Chinese pork sausage
3 ounces grated pared fresh ginger
  root
2 tablespoons soy sauce
2 tablespoons peanut oil
1½ tablespoons oyster sauce
1 tablespoon sesame oil
1½ cups long-grain white rice
1¾ cups plus 2 tablespoons water
2 tablespoons fresh coriander
  leaves

1. Cut each chicken thigh crosswise into 3 pieces. Cut sausages diagonally into ¼-inch slices.

2. Combine chicken, sausage, ginger, 1 tablespoon of the soy sauce, 1 tablespoon of the peanut oil, the oyster sauce and sesame oil in glass bowl. Marinate, covered, at room temperature, stirring occasionally, 1 hour.

3. Rinse rice thoroughly in sieve under cold running water; drain well.

4. Combine rice and water in large saucepan or 3-quart flameproof casserole. Heat, covered, over medium heat to boiling. Reduce heat to low; cook, covered, until water is approximately ⅔ absorbed, about 4 minutes. Turn heat off.

5. Quickly spoon chicken, sausage and marinade over rice in even layer. Cook, covered, over low heat 25 minutes. Remove pan from heat; do not uncover. Let stand 20 minutes.

6. Remove chicken and sausage to serving platter. Drizzle rice with remaining 1 tablespoon soy sauce and 1 tablespoon peanut oil; stir gently. Garnish with coriander leaves; serve with rice.                    *Makes 4 servings*

# Chicken Chow Mein

Fried Noodles (recipe follows)
2 whole boneless skinless chicken breasts
8 ounces lean boneless pork
2½ tablespoons dry sherry
2 tablespoons soy sauce
3 teaspoons cornstarch
2 medium yellow onions
1 red or green bell pepper
2 stalks celery
8 green onions
4 ounces cabbage
1 piece (1 inch square) fresh ginger root
8 ounces medium shrimp
2 tablespoons vegetable oil
1 clove garlic, crushed through press
½ cup water
2 teaspoons instant chicken bouillon granules

1. Prepare Fried Noodles.

2. Cut chicken and pork into 1-inch pieces. Blend ½ tablespoon each of the sherry and soy sauce and 1 teaspoon of the cornstarch in large bowl. Mix in chicken and pork. Cover and let stand 1 hour.

3. Peel and chop yellow onions. Remove seeds from pepper and cut into thin slices. Cut celery into 1-inch diagonal slices. Chop green onions. Shred cabbage. Pare ginger root and chop finely. Leaving tails intact, remove shells and back veins from shrimp.

4. Heat oil in wok over high heat. Stir-fry ginger and garlic in the oil for 1 minute. Add chicken and pork. Stir-fry over high heat until pork is no longer pink, 5 minutes.

5. Add shrimp to chicken mixture. Stir-fry until shrimp is done, 3 minutes longer.

6. Add all prepared vegetables to chicken mixture. Cook and stir until vegetables are crisp-tender, 3 to 5 minutes.

7. Combine water, bouillon, remaining 2 teaspoons cornstarch, 2 tablespoons sherry and 1½ tablespoons soy sauce. Pour mixture over chicken-vegetable mixture in wok. Cook and stir until sauce boils and thickens. Cook and stir 1 minute longer.

8. Arrange noodles on serving plate. Spoon Chow Mein over noodles.

*Makes 6 servings*

## Fried Noodles
8 ounces Chinese-style thin egg noodles
Water
Salt
3 cups vegetable oil

1. Cook noodles in boiling salted water according to package directions just until tender. Drain well.

2. Arrange several layers of paper towels over jelly roll pan or cookie sheet. Spread noodles evenly over paper towels. Let dry 2 to 3 hours.

3. Heat oil in wok over medium-high heat until it reaches 375°F.

4. Using long-handled tongs or slotted spoon, cook small amount of noodles at a time in oil until golden, about 30 seconds.

5. Remove noodles from oil. Drain on paper towels. Repeat to cook remaining noodles.

*Makes about 4 servings*

# Deep-Fried Marinated Chicken

(Toriniku Tasuta-Age)

1 teaspoon fresh ginger juice
½ small clove garlic, minced
1 tablespoon soy sauce
1 tablespoon saké
1 pound boneless skinless chicken
    breast
4 small green bell peppers
⅔ cup cornstarch
3 cups vegetable oil
    Lemon wedges (optional)

1. For marinade, mix ginger juice, garlic, soy sauce and saké in medium glass bowl; reserve.

2. Cut chicken into 1½-inch-square pieces. Add chicken to marinade, stirring to coat evenly; let stand 20 minutes.

3. Cut each green pepper in half lengthwise; cut halves crosswise into 1½-inch-wide strips.

4. Drain chicken; toss lightly in cornstarch to coat evenly. Shake off excess cornstarch.

5. Heat oven to 200°F. Heat oil in wok over high heat to 325°F. Add green peppers to wok; fry 30 seconds. Remove from oil with slotted spoon or strainer; drain on paper towels. Keep peppers warm in oven while cooking chicken.

6. Reheat oil to 325°F. Add 4 or 5 chicken pieces, 1 at a time, to wok; fry, turning occasionally, until golden and cooked through, 4 to 5 minutes. Remove from oil with slotted spoon; drain on paper towels. Place in warm oven. Reheat oil and repeat, frying 4 or 5 pieces at a time, until remaining chicken is cooked.

7. Arrange chicken and green peppers on serving platter or 4 individual plates; serve immediately, with lemon wedges.          *Makes 4 servings*

# Rolled Chicken and Green Onions

(Toriniku Negi-Maki)

2 large (7 to 8 ounces each)
    boneless whole chicken legs
    (drumsticks with thighs
    attached)
1 teaspoon fresh ginger juice
½ cup plus 2 tablespoons saké
1½ tablespoons sugar
2 tablespoons soy sauce
1 small leek, white part only
2 cups water
6 to 8 green onions
1½ tablespoons cornstarch
1 tablespoon vegetable oil

1. Pierce skin of each chicken piece several times with fork. Place chicken, skin side down, on work surface. Score thickest parts of meat with sharp knife; press and spread lightly so that meat is of even thickness.

2. Mix together ginger juice, 2 tablespoons saké, the sugar and soy sauce in medium bowl. Add chicken, turning to coat evenly; marinate 20 minutes, turning occasionally.

3. Cut leek crosswise into 2-inch lengths; cut each piece lengthwise in half and then into needle-fine strips. Soak in the water 5 minutes; drain and reserve.

4. Drain chicken reserving marinade; place chicken, skin side down, on cutting board. Cut onions to same length as long dimension of chicken pieces. Sift light, even coating of cornstarch over onions and chicken.

5. Place 3 or 4 onions across length of each chicken piece; roll each piece jelly-roll fashion around onions. Fasten each roll securely by wrapping with kitchen twine at ½-inch intervals.

6. Heat oil in 10-inch skillet over medium-high heat. Add chicken rolls, seam side down (to seal seam); cook, turning frequently with tongs, until light brown on all sides. Pour off excess fat.

7. Add remaining ½ cup saké to chicken. Reduce heat to medium-low; cook, covered, 7 minutes. Add reserved marinade; cook, covered, turning rolls occasionally, until chicken is tender, 10 to 12 minutes. Remove twine from rolls; cut crosswise into 1-inch-thick slices. Spoon pan juices over slices; serve with leek.

*Makes 4 servings*

# Green Curry of Chicken

Rich and Thin Coconut Milk
(see page 173)
Green Curry Paste (recipe
follows)
2 long thin Oriental eggplants
(about ¾ pound total weight)
1 or 2 hot fresh green chili peppers
1 broiler-fryer chicken (2½ to 3
pounds), cut into serving
pieces
2 tablespoons fish sauce
½ teaspoon salt
6 dried citrus leaves
3 tablespoons finely chopped fresh
coriander leaves
Hot cooked rice

1. Prepare Rich and Thin Coconut Milk. Combine both extractions in bowl; refrigerate, covered, at least 3 hours. Skim off thick coconut cream that has risen to top; measure and reserve ¾ cup. Measure and reserve 4 cups of the remaining coconut milk.

2. Prepare Green Curry Paste.

3. Cut eggplants crosswise at 1½-inch intervals. Seed chilies; cut lengthwise into thin slivers.

4. Heat reserved ¾ cup thick coconut cream in Dutch oven over high heat to boiling. Reduce heat to medium-high; cook, stirring constantly, until cream is reduced by half and oil separates out, 3 to 5 minutes. Stir in Green Curry Paste; stir-fry until paste is fragrant and oil separates, 3 to 5 minutes.

5. Add chicken. Cook over medium heat, stirring, turning and basting chicken frequently, until chicken is golden (not brown), 10 to 15 minutes.

6. Add eggplant, reserved 4 cups coconut milk, fish sauce, salt and citrus leaves; mix well. Heat to simmering; simmer, uncovered, over medium-low heat, stirring frequently, until chicken is tender and oil rises to surface of sauce, about 35 minutes. Stir in coriander and chilies; simmer 5 minutes. Remove and discard citrus leaves. Serve with rice. *Makes 4 servings*

1

3

5

## Green Curry Paste

5 stalks fresh lemon grass
6 hot fresh green chili peppers,
seeded and finely chopped
¼ cup minced shallots
2 tablespoons chopped fresh
coriander leaves and stems
3 cloves garlic, chopped
2 teaspoons dried shrimp paste
1 teaspoon ground turmeric
1 teaspoon ground cumin
1 teaspoon laos powder
1 teaspoon salt
1 teaspoon ground black pepper
¼ cup water

1. Trim root end of lemon grass. Cut off tapering upper green leaf portion, leaving about 5-inch long bulbous stalk. Peel off outer layers of bulbous stalk. Discard all trimmings. Mince remaining tender bulbous part of stalks.

2. Combine lemon grass with remaining ingredients except water in food processor or blender. Process, scraping down sides of container occasionally, until mixed. With motor running, add water in slow stream; continue processing, scraping occasionally, until pureed to a smooth paste, about 6 minutes. *Makes about 1 cup*

1

1       2       4       6

# Chicken with Soybeans

(Tori To Daizu Nimono)

**10 ounces dried soybeans
(about 2 cups)**
**1½ quarts water**
  **2 cups cold water**
   **Boiling water, if needed**
  **1 pound chicken wings***
  **5 tablespoons soy sauce**
  **3 tablespoons saké**
  **1 small leek**
  **1 piece (½ inch cube) pared fresh
ginger root**
  **1 tablespoon vegetable oil**
  **1 tablespoon sugar**

1. Rinse soybeans. Place beans in 1½ quarts water in large kettle; soak 12 hours.

2. Heat beans and soaking water to full boiling over high heat; add ½ cup cold water. Repeat 3 times.

3. Reduce heat to medium-low; simmer until beans are tender, about 1 hour. Beans should be covered with water during cooking; add boiling water, if necessary, to maintain proper level. Skim foam occasionally during cooking.

4. Meanwhile, place chicken wings in medium bowl; sprinkle with 1 tablespoon each soy sauce and saké. Let stand 20 minutes, turning wings occasionally.

5. Cut leek into 1-inch lengths. Cut ginger into ¹⁄₁₆-inch-thick slices.

6. Heat oil in heavy, 4 quart saucepan over medium-high heat. Add ginger; saute 30 seconds. Add chicken; saute until light brown on all sides, 6 to 8 minutes. Add leek; cook 2 minutes. Remove from heat.

7. Drain cooked beans, reserving cooking liquid. Add beans to chicken. Add enough cooking liquid to cover chicken and beans; stir in sugar. Heat over medium-high heat to boiling. Reduce heat to medium-low; simmer 5 minutes. Add remaining ¼ cup soy sauce and 2 tablespoons saké. Simmer until chicken is tender, about 20 minutes. *Makes 4 to 6 servings*

*Use whole wings or just middle sections and wing-tips.

# Chicken in Sweet Ginger Sauce

(Ga Rang Gang)

4 chicken legs (thighs and
    drumsticks attached)
    (about 2½ pounds)
1 large onion
2 cloves garlic
1 piece (2×1 inch) pared fresh
    ginger root
3 tablespoons vegetable oil
3 tablespoons sugar
⅛ teaspoon ground black pepper
3 tablespoons nuoc mam (fish
    sauce)
    Fresh Red Chili Flower*
    (optional)

1. Cut chicken legs crosswise with cleaver, using hacking motion, into 1-inch pieces.

2. Cut onion crosswise into ⅛-inch slices. Cut garlic into ¹⁄₁₆-inch slices. Cut ginger lengthwise into ⅛-inch slices, then cut slices lengthwise into ¹⁄₁₆-inch strips.

3. Heat oil in wok over high heat until hot, about 30 seconds. Reduce heat to

medium. Stir-fry onion, garlic and ginger until brown but not burned, 7 to 8 minutes.

4. Stir-fry chicken pieces, adding ¼ at a time, until very brown, about 10 minutes.

5. Sprinkle chicken with sugar and ground pepper; mix well. Cook, covered, over low heat, stirring occasionally to prevent sticking, until chicken is tender, 10 to 12 minutes

6. Add nuoc mam; mix well. Increase heat to medium; cook and stir until sauce is slightly thickened and chicken is coated, about 3 minutes. Immediately transfer to deep serving dish. Garnish with drained chili flower.

*Makes 4 servings*

*To make Fresh Red Chili Flower, cut long thin fresh red chili lengthwise, starting ½ inch from stem end, into 6 or 8 petals; discard seeds. Place chili in small bowl with ice water to cover. Refrigerate 1 hour.

# Lemon Chicken

4 whole chicken breasts
½ cup cornstarch
½ teaspoon salt
⅛ teaspoon pepper
¼ cup water
4 large egg yolks, slightly beaten
3 cups vegetable oil
4 green onions, sliced
1½ cups water
½ cup lemon juice
3½ tablespoons packed light brown sugar
3 tablespoons cornstarch
3 tablespoons honey
2 teaspoons instant chicken bouillon granules
1 teaspoon grated pared fresh ginger root

1. Remove skin from chicken and discard. Cut breasts in half. Remove and discard bones. Pound chicken breasts lightly with mallet or rolling pin.

2. Combine cornstarch, salt and pepper in small bowl. Gradually blend in water and egg yolks.

3. Pour oil into wok. Heat over high heat until oil reaches 375°F. Dip chicken breasts, one at a time, into cornstarch-egg yolk mixture. Fry breasts, two or three at a time, in hot oil until golden, about 5 minutes. Drain breasts on paper towels. Keep warm while cooking remaining chicken.

4. Cut each breast into three or four pieces and arrange on serving plate. Sprinkle with onions.

5. For sauce, combine remaining ingredients in medium saucepan. Stir until blended. Cook over medium heat, stirring constantly, until sauce boils and thickens, about 5 minutes. Pour over chicken.

*Makes 4 to 6 servings*

# Chicken with Broccoli and Cashews

1 teaspoon salt
½ teaspoon sugar
¼ teaspoon five-spice powder
1 pound boneless skinless chicken breasts, cut into ½-inch cubes
1 tablespoon rice wine
1 tablespoon cornstarch
1 teaspoon soy sauce
1 teaspoon sesame oil
12 ounces fresh broccoli, trimmed
1 cup peanut oil
4 ounces raw cashews
3 tablespoons cold water
1 teaspoon water chestnut flour
¾ cup chicken broth
1 teaspoon minced pared fresh ginger root
1 teaspoon minced garlic
¼ teaspoon ground white pepper

1. Sprinkle salt, sugar and five-spice powder over chicken in medium bowl; rub seasonings into chicken with fingertips. Mix rice wine, cornstarch, soy sauce and sesame oil in small bowl; pour over chicken and mix well. Marinate at room temperature 30 minutes.

2. Cut broccoli florets into 1¼-inch pieces. Cut broccoli stems lengthwise into ¼-inch pieces, then cut crosswise into 1¼-inch pieces.

3. Heat peanut oil in wok over high heat until very hot but not smoking. (To test, drop 1 cashew into oil; if it sizzles and turns golden in 3 seconds, oil is hot enough.) Add cashews to oil; fry until golden, about 5 seconds. Remove cashews with slotted spoon; drain on paper towels.

4. Remove oil from wok and reserve. Stir water and water chestnut flour in small bowl until smooth. Heat chicken broth in small saucepan over high heat to boiling.

5. Heat 3 tablespoons of the reserved oil in wok over high heat until hot, about 30 seconds. Stir-fry broccoli, adding ⅓ at a time, until crisp-tender, about 1 minute after all broccoli is added. Remove to plate with slotted spoon.

6. Add as much of the oil to wok as needed to make 3 tablespoons. Heat over medium heat until hot, about 10 seconds. Add ginger; stir-fry 10 seconds. Add garlic; stir-fry 5 seconds. Increase heat to high. Stir-fry chicken, adding ⅓ at a time, until cubes separate and begin to turn white, about 1 minute after all chicken is added.

7. Add broth and pepper to wok; cook and stir over high heat until boiling. Quickly stir water chestnut flour mixture; add to center of wok. Cook and stir until sauce thickens, about 30 seconds. Stir in broccoli; cook 10 seconds. Stir in cashews. Serve immediately.

*Makes 3 to 4 servings*

1

3

5

6

# Honey Chili Chicken

1 broiler-fryer chicken
   (about 3 pounds)
½ cup all-purpose flour
½ teaspoon salt
3 cups vegetable oil
⅓ cup water
⅓ cup lemon juice
2 teaspoons cornstarch
4 teaspoons Chinese chili sauce
2 teaspoons soy sauce
1½ teaspoons grated pared fresh
   ginger root
3 tablespoons honey
6 green onions, cut into thin
   lengthwise slices

1. Remove giblets from chicken. Rinse chicken and cut into small serving-size pieces. Combine flour and salt. Coat chicken pieces with flour mixture.

2. Heat oil in wok over high heat until it reaches 375°F. Add chicken pieces, one at a time, to hot oil (cook only ⅓ of the pieces at a time). Cook until golden, about 5 minutes. Drain on paper towels. Repeat with remaining chicken.

3. Pour all but 1 tablespoon of the oil out of the wok. Combine water, lemon juice, cornstarch, chili sauce and soy sauce.

4. Add ginger to oil in wok. Stir-fry 1 minute. Add honey to ginger. Cook and stir 1 minute. Add cornstarch-chili mixture to honey and ginger. Cook and stir until mixture boils, about 1 minute.

5. Stir chicken pieces into chili mixture. Cook and stir until chicken is hot throughout, about 3 minutes. Stir in onions. Cook and stir 1 minute.

*Makes 4 to 6 servings*

# Chicken Stir-Fry with Radish

2 medium dried black Chinese
    mushrooms
    Hot water
1¼ pounds chicken thighs (about 5)
2 tablespoons plus 2 teaspoons rice
    wine
¾ teaspoon sugar
1 tablespoon cornstarch
6 ounces pickled radish, drained
6 ounces fresh white button
    mushrooms
1 tablespoon ground brown bean
    sauce
2 teaspoons soy sauce
¼ cup peanut oil
⅓ cup chopped green onions,
    white part only

1. Soak mushrooms in hot water until tender, 20 to 30 minutes. Strain and reserve 3 tablespoons of the soaking liquid.

2. To bone chicken thighs: Place thigh skin side down; probe with fingers to locate bone. Make 1 cut through the meat to the bone. Scrape meat away from bone with tip of knife, working from center out to ends of bone.

3. At ends of bone, scrape and pull meat away from bone, cartilage and tendons; detach meat with knife or scissors. Pull off and discard skin.

4. Dice chicken into ⅜-inch cubes. Mix chicken with 2 tablespoons rice wine and the sugar in medium bowl. Sprinkle with cornstarch; stir to mix well. Marinate at room temperature 30 minutes.

5. Dice pickled radish into ¼-inch cubes; soak in large bowl of cold water to remove excess salt, 20 minutes. Drain well. Clean and trim white mushrooms. Dice white and black mushrooms into ¼-inch cubes. Mix bean sauce, soy sauce, 2 teaspoons rice wine and the reserved mushroom soaking liquid in small bowl.

6. Heat wok over high heat 15 seconds; add peanut oil and heat until hot, about 30 seconds. Scatter in chicken ¼ at a time; stir-fry 30 seconds after all chicken is added. Scatter in white and black mushrooms; stir-fry 30 seconds. Add pickled radish; stir-fry 1 minute. Stir in bean sauce mixture and onions; cook and stir 15 seconds. Serve immediately.

*Makes 3 to 4 servings*

# Pang Pang Chicken

2 whole chicken breasts
    (about 14 ounces each)
1½ to 2 quarts boiling water
    Cold water
    Ice cubes
3 medium cucumbers, preferably
    unwaxed
¼ cup sesame paste
1 to 3 teaspoons sesame oil
3 tablespoons minced green onion,
    white part only
1 tablespoon sugar
2 teaspoons minced pared fresh
    ginger root
2 teaspoons Chinese black vinegar
¼ teaspoon minced garlic
    (optional)
2 tablespoons soy sauce
¼ to ½ teaspoon hot pepper oil
    (optional)

1. Rinse chicken; place in wok. Add boiling water to cover. Heat over high heat to boiling. Adjust heat to maintain strong simmer or low boil (about medium-low). Skim foam; cover wok. Cook until juices run clear when chicken is pierced in thickest part with a knife, 20 to 25 minutes. Turn chicken over after first 10 minutes.

2. Fill large bowl halfway with cold water. Add chicken. Quickly add ice cubes to cover; let stand 20 minutes. Remove chicken from water; pat dry. Wrap in plastic wrap; refrigerate at least 2 hours or overnight.

3. About 30 minutes before serving, cut cucumbers crosswise into 2½-inch lengths. Pound each piece fairly hard with flat side of cleaver; cucumber will split lengthwise into 3 or 4 pieces. Break pieces apart completely and remove seeds. Cut pieces lengthwise into ¼-inch-wide sticks. Arrange on dish.

4. Pull chicken meat away from bones in 1 piece, leaving skin intact. Cut chicken lengthwise into ¼-inch-thick slices; arrange overlapping on top of cucumbers.

5. Mix sesame paste and sesame oil in small bowl until smooth; amount of oil needed depends on thickness of sesame paste. Add onion, sugar, ginger, vinegar and garlic; drizzle with soy sauce and stir to mix well. Stir in hot pepper oil. Spoon sesame sauce over chicken. Serve immediately.

*Makes 4 to 6 servings*

# Kung Pao Chicken

1

4

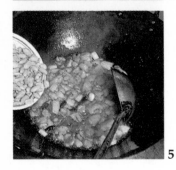

5

1¼ pounds chicken thighs (about 5)
 1 small egg
1½ tablespoons plus 2 teaspoons
      cornstarch
 4 tablespoons soy sauce
 4 tablespoons peanut oil
 1 can (19 ounces) bamboo shoots,
      rinsed and drained
 8 green onions, white part only
 3 to 5 dried red chili peppers,
      seeded
1½ tablespoons cold water
 2 tablespoons rice wine
1½ tablespoons Chinese black
      vinegar
 4 teaspoons sugar
 2 teaspoons sesame oil
 1 teaspoon minced pared fresh
      ginger root
 1 small clove garlic, minced
 1 cup unsalted roasted peanuts

1. Bone chicken thighs following directions in steps 2 and 3 of "Chicken
Stir-Fry with Radish" (see page 112);
remove and discard skin if desired.
Cut chicken into ¾-inch pieces. Beat
egg in medium bowl; add chicken.
Sprinkle with 1½ tablespoons cornstarch; mix well. Stir in 1 tablespoon
each soy sauce and peanut oil. Marinate at room temperature 30 minutes.

2. Cut bamboo shoots into ¾-inch
cubes. Cut onions into ¾-inch pieces.
Cut peppers into ½-inch pieces.

3. Mix 2 teaspoons cornstarch and the
water in small bowl until smooth. Stir
in 3 tablespoons soy sauce, the rice
wine, vinegar, sugar and sesame oil.

4. Heat wok over high heat 15 seconds; add remaining 3 tablespoons
peanut oil and heat until hot, about 30
seconds. Reduce heat to low. Add peppers; cook, stirring and pressing peppers against wok, until dark red, about
10 seconds. Add ginger and garlic;
stir-fry 10 seconds. Increase heat to
high. Scatter in chicken, about ¼ at a
time; stir-fry 1 minute after all chicken
has been added. Add bamboo shoots;
stir-fry 1 minute. Add onions; stir-fry
30 seconds.

5. Stir cornstarch mixture; add to wok.
Cook and stir until sauce thickens and
coats chicken evenly, about 30 seconds. Add peanuts and turn off heat;
stir mixture 2 or 3 times. Serve immediately.          *Makes 4 servings*

# Duck with Pineapple

1 ready-to-cook duck
    (4 to 5 pounds)
1¼ cups water
6 tablespoons dry sherry
4½ tablespoons white vinegar
4½ tablespoons soy sauce
4 tablespoons American-style
    barbecue sauce
¼ teaspoon five-spice powder
1 small ripe pineapple
4 green onions (optional)
2 tablespoons vegetable oil
2 teaspoons grated pared fresh
    ginger root
1 clove garlic, crushed through
    press
1 tablespoon cornstarch
    Green Onion Curls (see page 24)

1. Rinse duck and place on rack in baking pan. Combine ½ cup of the water; 3 tablespoons each of the sherry, vinegar, soy sauce and barbecue sauce; and the five-spice powder. Pour mixture over duck. Roast duck uncovered in preheated 425°F oven, basting and turning frequently, until light brown, about 20 minutes. Reduce oven temperature to 350°F and roast duck, basting and turning frequently, 1 hour longer. Remove duck from oven. Cool completely.

2. Cut duck in half. Remove and discard backbone. Cut duck into small serving-size pieces.

3. Remove top leaves and all skin from pineapple. Cut pineapple into quarters. Cut out and discard core. Cut pineapple quarters crosswise into ¼-inch slices. Cut onions into thin diagonal slices.

4. Heat oil in wok over high heat. Stir-fry ginger and garlic in the oil 1 minute. Add duck and stir-fry until duck is hot throughout, 3 to 4 minutes. Combine remaining ¾ cup water, 3 tablespoons sherry, 1½ tablespoons each vinegar and soy sauce, 1 tablespoon barbecue sauce and the cornstarch. Pour mixture over duck. Cook and stir until liquid boils. Add pineapple pieces and onions. Cook and stir until pineapple is hot, about 2 minutes longer. Garnish with Green Onion Curls. *Makes 6 servings*

# Braised Spiced Duck

1 whole duck (about 4½ pounds)
1 tablespoon five-spice powder
1 piece (1½×1 inch) pared fresh
    ginger root
1½ cups sugar
5 small star anise
1 piece (3 inches) cinnamon stick
4 cups water
1 tablespoon salt
2 to 3 teaspoons rice vinegar
    (optional)
1 tomato

1. Discard any visible fat from duck. Rub duck inside and out with five-spice powder. Let stand, uncovered, at room temperature 30 minutes.

2. Lightly pound ginger with flat side of cleaver to smash slightly.

3. Heat wok over high heat 30 seconds; reduce heat to medium. Add sugar; cook, stirring constantly, until sugar is almost completely melted and golden, about 5 minutes.

4. Add ginger, star anise and cinnamon to wok; stir-fry 30 seconds.

5. Add duck, breast side down; cook, spooning sugar over duck until breast side is brown, 1 to 2 minutes. Adjust heat to prevent sugar from burning. Turn duck over; cook, spooning sugar over duck, until second side is brown.

6. Stand back from wok and quickly add water; mixture may spatter. Add salt; heat over high heat to boiling. Reduce heat to low; simmer, covered, turning duck over every 20 minutes, until fork-tender, about 1½ hours. Remove duck; let stand 10 minutes.

7. Meanwhile, strain and degrease 2 cups of the cooking liquid. Heat in small saucepan, uncovered, stirring constantly, until sauce is reduced to 1⅓ cups, about 8 minutes. Remove from heat; stir in vinegar.

8. Cut wings and legs from duck. Separate back from breast portion; cut back crosswise into 4 pieces. Cut breast crosswise into 1¼-inch pieces.

9. Cut tomato into decorative shape. Reassemble duck on serving platter; pour ½ of the sauce over duck. Garnish with tomato. Serve immediately with remaining sauce.

*Makes 4 to 6 servings*

# SEAFOOD

# Stir-Fried Shrimp and Vegetables

8 small dried black Chinese
  mushrooms
  Boiling water
½ small head cauliflower (about
  10 ounces)
12 to 14 ounces broccoli
4 ounces fresh snow peas
1 medium carrot
2 quarts water
¼ cup chicken broth
2 tablespoons soy sauce
1½ tablespoons rice wine
2 teaspoons cornstarch
1 teaspoon sugar
5 tablespoons peanut oil
2 tablespoons minced green onion,
  white part only
2 teaspoons minced pared fresh
  ginger root
1 to 2 cloves garlic, minced
¾ pound medium shrimp, shelled,
  deveined, tails intact

1. Place mushrooms in bowl and cover with boiling water. Let soak 30 minutes. Drain. Trim and discard stems; squeeze out excess water.

2. Cut cauliflower into 1-inch florets. Cut broccoli florets from stem. Cut florets into 1-inch pieces. Pare thick stems; slant-cut into ¼-inch slices.

3. Remove stems and strings from snow peas. Cut out 4 evenly spaced narrow wedges lengthwise from carrot, then cut crosswise into ⅛-inch slices.

4. Heat 2 quarts water in large saucepan over high heat to boiling. Add carrot pieces; cook 1 minute. Remove carrot pieces; drain well. Repeat blanching procedure with cauliflower, then with broccoli, blanching each 1 minute. Repeat procedure with snow peas, blanching only 30 seconds. Pat vegetables dry with paper towels.

5. Mix broth, soy sauce, rice wine, cornstarch and sugar in small bowl.

6. Heat oil in wok over high heat until hot, about 30 seconds. Reduce heat to low; stir-fry onion, ginger and garlic 10 seconds. Increase heat to high; stir-fry mushrooms 30 seconds.

7. Stir-fry shrimp, adding ⅓ at a time, about 1 minute after all shrimp are added. Add broccoli; stir-fry 30 seconds. Add cauliflower; stir-fry 30 seconds. Add snow peas and carrots; stir-fry 30 seconds.

8. Quickly stir broth mixture; add to wok. Cook and stir until thickened, about 30 seconds. Serve immediately.
*Makes 4 servings*

# Crawfish with Black Bean Sauce

6 small whole fresh crawfish
   (spiny or rock lobsters) or
   thawed frozen crawfish tails
   (4 to 5 ounces each)
2 tablespoons fermented black
   beans
1 tablespoon minced green onion
2 cloves garlic, minced
1 teaspoon minced pared fresh
   ginger root
⅔ cup water
2 tablespoons soy sauce
2 tablespoons rice wine
¼ cup peanut oil
1½ teaspoons sugar
   Fresh coriander sprigs

1. Detach and discard crawfish heads. Using scissors, cut along both sides of underside of shell. Pull off and discard this portion of shell.

2. Rinse beans in small sieve under cold running water; drain well. Lightly pound beans with flat side of cleaver to slightly smash.

3. Combine onion, garlic and ginger in small bowl. Mix water, soy sauce and rice wine in second small bowl.

4. Heat oil in large skillet or wok over medium heat until hot, about 45 seconds. Add onion mixture; stir-fry 10 seconds. Add beans and sugar; stir-fry 10 seconds. Add crawfish; stir-fry 30 seconds.

5. Cover skillet; steam-cook crawfish 2 minutes. Uncover skillet; increase heat to high. Add soy sauce mixture; cook and stir until crawfish are opaque and sauce is slightly thickened, about 8 minutes. Garnish with coriander sprigs. Serve immediately.

*Makes 6 servings*

1

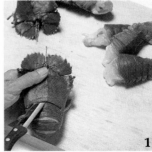
1

4

# Fried Chili Crabs

3 pounds fresh whole hard-shelled
   crabs*
2 ounces shallots, chopped
1 ounce chopped pared fresh
   ginger root
4 candlenuts or macadamia nuts,
   chopped
3 to 4 cloves garlic, chopped
2 long thin hot fresh red chili
   peppers, seeded and chopped
1 tablespoon preserved whole
   brown soybeans, drained
5 tablespoons vegetable oil
¼ cup catsup
2 tablespoons Oriental sweet chili
   sauce
2 teaspoons sugar
½ teaspoon salt
⅓ cup plus 2 tablespoons water
1 tablespoon cornstarch
1 large egg
   French bread

1. Pull hard body shell off each crab; reserve 1 or 2 shells for garnish if desired. Cut crabs in half lengthwise, pull off and discard gray spongy tissue. Cut off claws; pound lightly with back of cleaver or flat mallet to crack shells.

2. Pound shallots, ginger, nuts, garlic, chilies and soybeans together in mortar with pestle to fine paste. Or, combine in blender with 2 tablespoons of the oil and process to smooth paste.

3. Combine catsup, chili sauce, sugar and salt in small bowl; mix well. Mix 2 tablespoons of the water and the cornstarch in another small bowl until smooth; add egg and whisk until well blended.

4. Heat remaining oil in wok over high heat until hot. Reduce heat to me-dium; add shallot paste and stir-fry 2 minutes. Add crabs and reserved shells; stir to coat. Add catsup mixture; stir-fry 2 minutes. Stir in remaining ⅓ cup water. Reduce heat to medium-low; simmer, covered, 5 minutes.

5. Uncover wok; reduce heat to low. Stir in egg-cornstarch mixture; cook, stirring constantly, until sauce thickens, 1 to 2 minutes. Transfer to serving dish. Serve immediately with bread for soaking up sauce.

*Makes 4 to 6 servings*

*If fresh crabs are not available, substitute 2 pounds fresh prawns or jumbo shrimp. Shell and devein prawns, leaving tails intact. Decrease simmering time at end of Step 4 to 1 minute.

# Clams in Black Bean Sauce

24 small hard-shell clams
⅓ cup water
1½ tablespoons fermented black
    beans
 2 cloves garlic, minced
 1 teaspoon minced fresh ginger
    root
 2 tablespoons vegetable oil
 2 green onions, thinly sliced
 1 cup chicken broth
 2 tablespoons dry sherry
 1 tablespoon soy sauce
1½ to 2 cups Chinese-style thin egg
    noodles, cooked and drained
 3 tablespoons chopped fresh
    coriander leaves or 4 fresh
    parsley sprigs (optional)

1. Scrub clams under cold running water with stiff brush. (Discard any shells that do not close when tapped.)

2. Combine water and black beans in small bowl. Let stand 15 minutes. Drain beans, reserving 1 teaspoon of the water. Coarsely chop beans. Combine beans, reserved water, garlic and ginger on small plate; finely chop together.

3. Heat oil in Dutch oven over medium heat until hot. Add black bean mixture and onions; stir-fry 30 seconds. Add clams; stir to coat.

4. Add chicken broth, sherry and soy sauce. Heat over high heat to boiling. Reduce heat to low; simmer, covered, until clam shells open, 5 to 8 minutes. (Discard any clams that do not open.)

5. To serve, divide noodles equally among 4 large bowls. Arrange clams on top. Ladle broth over clams. Garnish each serving with chopped coriander or parsley sprigs.

*Makes 4 servings*

# Scallops with Vegetables

1 ounce dried black Chinese
　　mushrooms
　Boiling water
1 pound fresh or thawed frozen
　　sea scallops
2 medium yellow onions
3 stalks celery
8 ounces fresh green beans,
　　trimmed
6 green onions
4 teaspoons cornstarch
1 cup water
2½ tablespoons dry sherry
4 teaspoons soy sauce
2 teaspoons instant chicken
　　bouillon granules
2 tablespoons vegetable oil
2 teaspoons grated pared fresh
　　ginger root
1 clove garlic, crushed through
　　press
1 can (15 ounces) baby corn,
　　drained

1. Place mushrooms in bowl and cover with boiling water. Let stand 30 minutes. Drain. Squeeze out excess water. Cut into thin slices.

2. Rinse scallops; drain. Trim, if necessary, and cut into quarters.

3. Peel yellow onions, cut into wedges and separate layers. Cut celery into ½-inch diagonal slices. Cut green beans into 1-inch diagonal slices. Cut green onions into thin diagonal slices.

4. Measure cornstarch into small bowl. Blend in a few tablespoons of the water and mix until smooth. Stir in the remaining water, the sherry, soy sauce and bouillon.

5. Heat oil in wok over high heat. Add yellow onions, celery, beans, ginger and garlic to oil. Stir-fry 3 minutes.

Add cornstarch mixture to vegetable mixture. Cook and stir until mixture boils.

6. Add scallops, mushrooms, green onions and corn. Cook and stir until scallops are tender, about 4 minutes.

*Makes 4 to 6 servings*

# Salmon Teriyaki

(Sake Teriyaki)

**1 pound salmon steak or fillets**
**2 tablespoons soy sauce**
**1 tablespoon mirin**
**2 teaspoons saké**
**1 teaspoon sugar**
**3 ounces daikon, pared**
**1 tablespoon vegetable oil**

1. Cut salmon into 4 equal pieces; place in shallow glass bowl.

2. Mix soy sauce, mirin, saké and sugar in small bowl; stir to dissolve sugar. Pour marinade over salmon; let stand 10 minutes. Drain salmon, reserving marinade.

3. Grate daikon; drain (but do not squeeze).

4. To fry: Heat oil in 8- or 10-inch skillet over medium heat. Add salmon; cook until light brown, 2 to 3 minutes. Gently turn salmon over; cook just until salmon is cooked through and flakes easily with fork, about 2 minutes. Reduce heat to low. Add marinade; cook just until salmon pieces are well coated and sauce is hot, about 1 minute.

5. To broil: Heat broiler; brush broiler rack with oil. Place salmon on rack; brush lightly with marinade. Broil about 4 inches from heat source until light brown, 5 to 6 minutes. Turn salmon pieces; brush lightly with marinade. Broil just until salmon is cooked through and flakes easily with fork, 5 to 6 minutes.

6. Serve immediately with grated daikon and pan juices from skillet.

*Makes 4 servings*

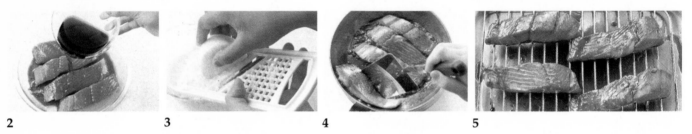

2  3  4  5

# Teriyaki Scallops

(Hotategai Teriyaki)

**2 tablespoons soy sauce**
**1 tablespoon mirin**
**2 teaspoons saké**
**1 teaspoon sugar**
**1 pound large scallops (trimmed, if desired)**
**8 ounces asparagus**
**2½ cups water**
**¼ teaspoon salt**
**1 tablespoon vegetable oil**

1. Mix soy sauce, mirin, saké and sugar in medium bowl; stir to dissolve sugar. Add scallops; let stand 10 minutes, turning occasionally. Drain scallops, reserving marinade.

2. Cut asparagus spears in half crosswise. Heat water and salt to boiling in 2-quart saucepan over high heat; add asparagus. Reduce heat to medium-high; boil gently until crisp-tender, 3 to 5 minutes. Drain; keep warm.

3. To fry scallops: Heat oil in 8- or 10-inch skillet over medium heat. Add scallops; cook until light brown, about 2 minutes. Turn scallops over; cook just until opaque in center and cooked through, 1 to 2 minutes. Reduce heat to low. Add marinade; cook just until scallops are well coated and sauce is hot, about 1 minute.

4. To broil scallops: Heat broiler; brush broiler rack with oil. Place scallops on rack; brush lightly with marinade. Broil about 4 inches from heat source until brown, 4 to 5 minutes. Turn scallops; brush lightly with marinade. Broil just until scallops are opaque in center and cooked through, 4 to 5 minutes. Do not overcook.

5. Serve immediately with asparagus; pass pan juices from skillet.

*Make 4 servings*

1  3  4

# Hot and Sweet Squid

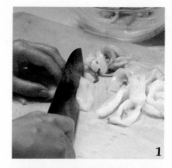

1½ pounds cleaned squid
1 large carrot
1 medium onion
1 small green bell pepper
4 hot fresh red chili peppers
½ cup soy sauce
1 tablespoon sugar
1 tablespoon sesame oil
1 tablespoon sesame seeds, toasted
3 to 4 cloves garlic, crushed
    through press
2½ tablespoons Korean red pepper
    powder* (optional)
2 tablespoons vegetable oil

1. Rinse squid; drain well. Cut tentacle clusters into 2 or 3 smaller clusters; slant-cut bodies crosswise into ¼-inch rings.

2. Cut carrot into 1½×¼×⅛-inch pieces. Cut onion in half lengthwise; cut halves lengthwise into ⅛-inch slices. Cut green pepper into 1½×¼-inch pieces.

3. Cut chilies in half lengthwise; remove and discard seeds. Cut chilies into 1½×¼-inch pieces.

4. Add soy sauce, sugar, sesame oil, sesame seeds and garlic to squid in large bowl; mix well. Stir in red pepper powder; marinate at room temperature, stirring occasionally, 1 hour.

5. Heat vegetable oil in medium, deep skillet over medium-high heat until hot. Add carrot, onion, green pepper and chilies; cook and stir 3 minutes. Reduce heat to medium; add squid mixture. Cook, stirring constantly, just until squid is cooked, 3 to 4 minutes; do not overcook or squid will be tough. Serve immediately.

*Makes 4 servings*

*This is a very hot dish; decrease red pepper powder if desired.

2                     3                     4

# Miso Mackerel

(Saba Miso-Ni)

**2 thick mackerel fillets\***
    **(about 8 ounces each)**
**2 medium leeks**
**1 cube (1 inch) pared fresh ginger**
    **root**
**1 cup water**
**1½ tablespoons saké**
**1½ tablespoons soy sauce**
**1½ teaspoons mirin**
**1½ tablespoons sugar**
**3 tablespoons red or brown miso**

1. Remove any bones from fillets. Cut each fillet in half crosswise.

2. Cut leeks into 1½-inch lengths. Cut ginger into ¹⁄₁₆-inch-thick slices. Stack ½ of the ginger slices and cut into ¹⁄₁₆-inch-wide strips; reserve strips for garnish.

3. Combine water, saké, soy sauce, mirin and sugar in 3-quart saucepan; heat to simmering over high heat. Add sliced ginger; place fish, skin side up, in saucepan in single layer. Heat to boiling; cook 3 minutes.

4. Reduce heat to medium-high; baste fish thoroughly with cooking liquid. Add leeks; boil fish and leeks, basting several times, until fish is cooked though and flakes easily with a fork, 5 to 7 minutes. Remove fish and leeks from pan; place on 4 serving plates, dividing evenly.

5. Add miso to cooking liquid; stir well to dissolve miso. Heat over medium-high heat to boiling; cook until sauce thickens slightly, 2 to 4 minutes.

6. Pour desired amount of sauce over fish; top with reserved ginger strips.
*Makes 4 servings*

\*Substitute yellowtail, herring, shad or similar round-bodied, somewhat fatty fish, if desired.

# Salmon-Tofu Balls

(Sake Tofu Agedango)

12 ounces salmon fillets or steaks
 5 cups water
½ teaspoon saké
½ teaspoon plus pinch salt
10 ounces tofu
⅓ cup plus 2½ tablespoons all-
  purpose flour
½ teaspoon sugar
¼ cup soy sauce
 4 teaspoons grated pared fresh
  ginger root
 4 to 6 leaves green or red leaf
  lettuce
 3 to 4 cups vegetable oil

**1**

**1**

1. Place salmon, 2 cups water, the saké and pinch of salt in 2-quart saucepan; heat over medium-high heat to boiling. Reduce heat to medium; boil gently just until fish is cooked through and flakes easily with fork, about 3 minutes. Drain; remove skin and bones, if any. Flake salmon; chop finely.

2. Cut tofu crosswise into 5 or 6 equal pieces. Place tofu and remaining 3 cups water in 2-quart saucepan. Heat to boiling over medium-high heat; boil 2 minutes. Transfer tofu to cloth-lined sieve; drain well.

3. Wrap cloth around tofu; wring or squeeze firmly to remove as much moisture as possible. Using fork, break tofu into small pieces.

4. Place salmon and tofu in medium bowl; sprinkle with 2½ tablespoons flour, the sugar and remaining ½ teaspoon salt. Mix thoroughly. Shape into 1½-inch balls. Lightly roll each ball in remaining ⅓ cup flour; shake off excess flour.

5. For dipping sauce: Place 1 tablespoon soy sauce in each of 4 small bowls; place 1 teaspoon ginger in center of each bowl. Each person mixes ginger with soy sauce, as desired.

6. Arrange lettuce leaves in serving bowl.

7. Heat oil to 325°F in wok, deep fryer or deep, heavy saucepan. Add 5 or 6 salmon balls, 1 at a time, to hot oil; turn immediately. Fry balls until golden, turning occasionally, 3 to 4 minutes. Remove from oil with slotted spoon; drain on paper towels. Reheat oil to 325°F; repeat with remaining salmon balls.

8. Place salmon balls on lettuce leaves. Serve immediately with dipping sauce.     *Makes 4 servings*

**2**

**3**

**4**

**7**

# Tuna Teriyaki
(Maguro Teriyaki)

1½ **pounds fresh tuna fillets, ¾ inch thick***
¼ **cup soy sauce**
2 **tablespoons saké**
1 **tablespoon sugar**
½ **teaspoon minced pared fresh ginger root (optional)**
¼ **teaspoon minced garlic (optional)**
1½ **tablespoons vegetable oil**
2 **small limes, cut into halves**
4 **sticks pickled ginger (optional)**

1. Cut tuna into 4 equal pieces; place in single layer in shallow bowl.

2. Combine soy sauce, saké, sugar, minced ginger and garlic in small bowl; stir until sugar is dissolved.

3. Pour soy marinade over tuna. Marinate at room temperature, turning frequently, 40 minutes.

4. Drain tuna, reserving marinade. Heat oil in large skillet over medium heat until hot.** Add tuna; cook until light brown, 2 to 3 minutes. Turn tuna over; cook just until opaque, 2 to 3 minutes.

5. Reduce heat to medium-low; pour reserved marinade over tuna. Add limes to skillet, cut side down. Cook, carefully turning tuna once, until coated and sauce is hot, 1 to 1½ minutes.

6. Serve immediately with limes and pickled ginger.          *Makes 4 servings*

*Substitute salmon, halibut, swordfish or other firm-fleshed fish if desired.

**Fish can be cooked over charcoal or broiled if desired. Add oil to marinade in Step 2. Grill or broil fish 4 inches from heat until light brown, 2 to 3 minutes. Gently turn fish over; cook until opaque, 2 to 3 minutes. Brush with marinade; cook 20 to 30 seconds. Gently turn fish over; brush with marinade and cook 20 to 30 seconds. Serve immediately with limes and pickled ginger.

# Fish Fillets in Tamarind Sauce

⅓ cup water
1 tablespoon tamarind extract
2 tablespoons soy sauce
2 tablespoons fish sauce
2 tablespoons dark brown sugar
6 green onions, white part only
1 fresh red chili pepper
4 red snapper fillets (7 to 8 ounces each)*
½ teaspoon salt
¼ teaspoon ground white pepper
2 tablespoons cornstarch
2 cups peanut oil
2 tablespoons minced pared fresh ginger root
6 cloves garlic, minced
3 tablespoons chopped fresh coriander leaves
  Slivered green onion tops
  Fresh Green Chili Flowers**
  (optional)

1. Mix water and tamarind extract in small bowl until dissolved. Stir in soy sauce, fish sauce and brown sugar until sugar is dissolved.

2. Cut white parts of green onions crosswise into ½-inch pieces. Seed red chili; cut lengthwise into thin slivers.

3. Pat fish dry with paper towels. Sprinkle fish on both sides with salt and white pepper. Sprinkle cornstarch through sieve over fish; coat both sides.

4. Heat oil in wok over high heat to 365°F. Adjust heat to maintain temperature.

5. Fry fish, 2 pieces at a time, tilting wok occasionally if needed to cover fish with oil, just until opaque, 2 to 3 minutes. Remove fish, draining well; keep warm, loosely covered.

6. Remove all but 2 tablespoons oil from wok. Add green onion pieces, ginger and garlic to wok; stir-fry over medium heat until fragrant but not brown, 5 to 10 seconds. Add tamarind mixture; cook and stir over high heat 30 seconds. Stir in coriander and slivered chili; pour sauce over fish on serving platter. Garnish with slivered green onion and Fresh Green Chili Flowers. Serve immediately.

*Makes 4 servings*

*If small fillets are not available, use a total of 1½ to 1¾ pounds fillets; cut into 4 even-sized pieces. Sea bass or halibut can be substituted for red snapper.

**To make Fresh Green Chili Flowers, make deep V-shaped cuts all around chili, starting ⅔ of the way from stem end. Pull 2 pieces apart. Remove and discard seeds.

2      3      5

# Spicy Pickled Fish

(Kinilaw)

1½ pounds fresh red snapper fillets,
    skinned
1½ cups white vinegar
  ¼ cup fresh lemon juice
  1 piece (1×½×½ inch) pared fresh
    ginger root
  2 fresh hot red chili peppers,
    seeded
  1 or 2 small red onions
1½ teaspoons salt
  ¼ teaspoon ground white pepper

1. Cut fish into 1-inch squares.

2. Combine fish, ¾ cup vinegar and the lemon juice in medium glass bowl; mix well. Refrigerate, covered, stirring occasionally, until fish is opaque throughout, about 4 hours.

3. Cut ginger lengthwise into ¹⁄₁₆-inch slices, then cut slices lengthwise into ¼-inch strips. Cut chilies lengthwise into ¼-inch strips, then cut strips crosswise into ¾-inch pieces.

4. Cut onions crosswise into ⅛-inch slices; separate slices into rings.

5. Just before serving, drain fish well. Transfer to serving bowl. Add remaining ¾ cup vinegar, the ginger, chilies, onion, salt and pepper; mix well.

*Makes 4 to 6 servings*

1                2                4

# Deep-Fried Fish Vinaigrette

(Sakana Nanban-Zuke)

1 medium yellow onion
1 piece (1½ inches) carrot, about
    1 inch in diameter
2 small green bell peppers
2 or 3 dried red chili peppers,
    seeded
¾ cup rice vinegar
3 tablespoons soy sauce
1 tablespoon sugar
½ teaspoon salt
8 to 10 small horse mackerel
    (4 to 6 inches long), heads and
    tails intact*
¾ cup all-purpose flour
3 to 4 cups vegetable oil
½ medium lemon, cut into thin
    slices

1. Cut onion crosswise into ⅛-inch-thick slices; separate slices into rings. Cut carrot crosswise into ¹⁄₁₆-inch-thick slices; if desired, cut slices into decorative shapes using knife or vegetable cutter. Cut green peppers crosswise into ⅛-inch-thick slices. Cut chilies in half crosswise.

2. Mix rice vinegar, soy sauce, sugar and salt in shallow, noncorrosive pan or glass dish large enough to accommodate fish in single layer; stir to dissolve sugar. Add carrots, chili peppers, green peppers and onions to pan; marinate at room temperature while preparing fish.

3. Coat fish lightly and evenly with flour; coat insides of fish with flour. Shake to remove excess flour.

4. Heat oil to 325°F in wok, deep fryer or deep, heavy saucepan. Slide fish into oil, one at a time; fry as many as will fit in single layer. Cook until golden, turning occasionally, 6 to 7 minutes. Remove fish from oil with slotted spoon; drain on paper towels. (If desired, cut off heads of fish.) Reheat oil to 325°F; repeat with remaining fish.

5. Add hot fish to vegetables in marinade. Marinate at room temperature 1 to 2 hours, turning fish occasionally.** Serve fish and vegetables garnished with lemon slices.

*Makes 4 servings*

*If unavailable, substitute large smelts or similar fish.

**This dish may be prepared 1 to 2 days in advance. Refrigerate, covered; allow to come to room temperature before serving.

# Steamed Whole Fish
# with Ginger and Chili

4 large dried black Chinese
   mushrooms
   Boiling water
1 piece (2×½×½ inch) pared fresh
   ginger root
2 long thin fresh red chili peppers,
   seeded
4 or 5 small green onions
1 whole fresh pomfret, pompano
   or red snapper (1½ to 2
   pounds), cleaned, at room
   temperature
¼ teaspoon salt
1½ teaspoons cornstarch
2 tablespoons rice wine
1 tablespoon soy sauce
1 tablespoon vegetable oil
2 tablespoons fresh coriander
   leaves

1. Place mushrooms in bowl and cover with boiling water. Let soak 30 minutes. Drain. Trim and discard stems; squeeze out excess water.

2. Cut mushrooms into ¼-inch-wide strips. Cut ginger lengthwise into 1/16-inch slices, then cut slices lengthwise into 1/16-inch shreds. Cut chilies lengthwise into ⅛-inch strips. Cut white part of green onions lengthwise into fine shreds; cut green part crosswise into 2-inch lengths.

3. Pat fish dry. Score both sides of fish at 1-inch intervals, cutting down to bone. Sprinkle each side of fish with salt and rub in; repeat with cornstarch. Place fish on large heatproof plate that will fit in wok on steaming rack.

4. Place white part of green onion in cavity of fish. Arrange mushroom strips around fish. Sprinkle ginger and chili shreds evenly over top of fish. Drizzle rice wine, soy sauce and oil over fish.

5. Place steaming rack in wok. Add boiling water to within 1 inch of rack. Place plate on steaming rack; cover wok. Adjust heat to maintain gentle but steady steam, about medium-low. Steam until fish is just opaque throughout, 15 to 20 minutes.

6. Fish can be served directly from plate used for steaming, or if desired, carefully transfer fish to heated serving platter, using 2 wide spatulas. Sprinkle green onion tops and coriander leaves around fish. Serve immediately.   *Makes 2 or 3 servings*

3              4              5

# Crisp-Coated Fried Fish

(Sakana Kawari-Age)

8 fresh sardines, horse mackerel or smelts (about 3 ounces each), tails intact
1 teaspoon salt
¼ cup Worcestershire sauce
¼ cup catsup
½ teaspoon prepared Japanese mustard
4 teaspoons fresh lemon juice
2 large eggs
2 tablespoons water
½ cup all-purpose flour
1 cup finely chopped peanuts or coarsely crushed corn flakes*
¾ to 1 cup white or black sesame seeds*
3 to 4 cups vegetable oil
4 lemon wedges

1. Using scissors, cut undersides of fish up to the tail sections; cut through backbones at tail ends. Gently pull out backbones; discard. Spread fish flat. Rinse fish under cold running water; drain. Pat dry with paper towels. Sprinkle fish with salt; let stand 10 minutes.

2. For dipping sauce, combine Worcestershire sauce, catsup, mustard and lemon juice in small bowl; stir to mix well. Reserve.

3. Beat eggs and water in small bowl. Place flour in shallow dish or on waxed paper. Place peanuts (or corn flakes) and white (or black) sesame seeds each in separate shallow dishes or on waxed paper.

4. Dip fish in flour to coat both sides evenly; shake to remove excess flour. Dip fish in egg mixture, then in coating, using peanuts for 4 fish and sesame seeds for remaining 4 fish. Press coating evenly onto both sides of fish. Let stand 5 minutes. Heat oven to 200°F.

5. Heat oil over high heat to 325°F in wok, deep fryer or deep, heavy saucepan. Adjust heat as necessary to maintain proper frying temperature. Fry 2 fish at a time: Slide each fish into oil, skin side up; fry 2 minutes. Turn fish over, fry just until fish is cooked through and coating is crisp, 1 to 2 minutes. Remove fish with tongs; drain on paper towels. Keep warm in oven. Reheat oil to 325°F and repeat with remaining fish.

6. Serve fish immediately with dipping sauce and lemon wedges.

*Makes 4 servings*

*Use from 1 to all 4 coating ingredients, as desired. Approximately ¼ cup coating is needed for each fish.

4

4

5

5

# Salt-Grilled Whole Fish

(Sakana Shio-Yaki)

1

2

3

4 whole horse mackerel
   (10 to 12 ounces each), heads
   and tails intact*
4 teaspoons salt
3 ounces daikon, pared
½ medium lime or lemon
1 tablespoon vegetable oil
4 teaspoons grated pared fresh
   ginger root
  Soy sauce (optional)

1. If fish is thick, make 1 or 2 diagonal cuts, about ½ inch deep, along side of body; repeat on second side of fish. Sprinkle 1 teaspoon salt over each fish, coating both sides; let stand 10 minutes. Wipe off salt with paper towels.

2. Grate daikon; drain well in sieve. Cut lime into thick slices or wedges.

3. Brush grill rack lightly with oil; heat rack over medium-hot charcoal fire.** Place fish on rack; grill until brown, 4 to 6 minutes. Carefully turn fish; grill until brown and fish flakes easily with fork, 3 to 5 minutes.

4. Carefully transfer each fish to serving plate. Place about 1½ tablespoons daikon topped with 1 teaspoon ginger on each plate; add lime slices. Serve immediately. Pass soy sauce to pour over fish.    *Makes 4 servings*

*Other firm, lean, white-fleshed fish can be used, for example, sea bream, sea bass or red snapper.

**Fish can broiled: Heat broiler; brush broiler rack with oil. Proceed as for grilling, increasing cooking time 1 to 2 minutes on each side of fish.

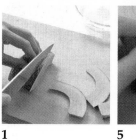

1

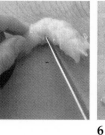

5

6

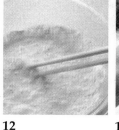

12

14

14. To cook mushrooms: Heat oil to 340°F. Spoon batter on underside of mushrooms only; shake off excess batter. Add mushrooms to oil, batter side down; fry, turning once, until mushrooms are tender, about 1 minute. Remove from oil; drain.

15. To cook green beans and carrot: Grasp each cluster and dredge in flour; shake off excess (or sprinkle flour lightly over clusters). Spoon batter to coat over each cluster. Carefully add each cluster to oil; fry, turning once, until golden, about 2 minutes. Remove from oil; drain.

16. To cook peas, green onions and small shrimp: Sprinkle flour lightly over peas; stir to coat peas. Spoon just enough batter over peas to coat; stir or toss gently. Place spoonful of mixture (1 to 2 tablespoons) in oil; using 2 spoons, quickly press into rounded shape. Repeat with remaining peas. Fry, turning once, until batter is crisp, 2 to 3 minutes. Remove from oil; drain. Heat oil to 360°F. Repeat procedure for onions and small shrimp combination.

17. To cook fish, squid and large shrimp: Dredge each piece in flour; shake off excess flour. Dip piece in bat-

ter; shake off excess. Slide each piece into oil (for fish, skin side up). Fry, turning once, until golden and crisp: for fish, about 3 minutes; for squid, about 1 minute; for shrimp, 3 to 4 minutes. Remove from oil; drain.

18. To serve, pour about ¼ cup warm dipping sauce into each small bowl of reserved daikon and ginger. Each person mixes daikon and ginger into sauce, as desired. Dip hot food into sauce. Pass lemon wedges and remaining warm sauce. (If desired, place paper towels on serving platter and plates.)                *Makes 4 servings*

# Seafood, Chicken and Vegetable Casserole

(Yosenabe)

8 ounces boneless chicken or boneless beef sirloin
8 ounces fish fillets or steaks, such as cod, sea bream, sea bass or salmon*
4 to 6 hard-shell clams*
3 quarts water
8½ teaspoons salt
4 large scallops (trimmed, if desired)*
6 ounces shucked oysters*
4 to 8 large shrimp, in shells*
8 medium fresh black Chinese mushrooms
4 leaves Chinese cabbage (napa or bok choy)
1 or 2 leeks
10 ounces tofu
1 large carrot, 1 to 1½ inches in diameter
8 ounces shirataki filaments
Ponzu sauce (see page 78)
6 tablespoons grated pared daikon, drained
Pinch cayenne pepper
1½ quarts Dashi (see page 48)
1 tablespoon mirin
1 tablespoon soy sauce
Boiling water, if needed
¼ cup sliced green onion

1. Cut chicken and fish fillets into 1¼-inch squares.

2. Place clams in medium bowl with 1 quart water and 4 teaspoons salt; let stand 15 to 20 minutes. Rinse well under cold running water; drain. Rinse scallops under cold running water; drain.

3. Place oysters in sieve; lower into 1 quart water mixed with 4 teaspoons salt in medium bowl. Soak 5 minutes. Rinse under cold running water; drain. Shell shrimp, leaving tail and section of shell nearest tail attached. Remove vein by inserting wooden pick under vein and lifting up gently.

4. Remove and discard stems from mushrooms; if desired, make shallow, V-shaped cuts in crisscross design on cap of each mushroom. Cut cabbage leaves into 2-inch squares. Cut leek diagonally into ½-inch-thick slices. Cut tofu into 1-inch cubes; drain.

5. Cut carrot crosswise into ¼-inch-thick slices. Heat remaining 1 quart water to boiling in 2-quart saucepan over high heat. Place carrot in sieve and lower into boiling water; cook 1 minute. Rinse under cold running water; drain. Add shirataki to boiling water; cook 2 minutes. Drain well; cut into 4-inch lengths.

6. Prepare Ponzu Sauce. Mix daikon with cayenne pepper in small bowl.

7. Place about ¼ each of the chicken, fish, shellfish, vegetables, shirataki and tofu in table-cooking utensil.** Use sufficient amounts to comfortably fill pot. Arrange remainder of these ingredients on platter.

8. Place Dashi, mirin, soy sauce and remaining ½ teaspoon salt in 3-quart saucepan; heat to boiling over medium-high heat.

9. At the table, pour sufficient boiling Dashi mixture over food in cooking pot to reach just below top of food. (Reserve any remaining Dashi mixture over very low heat.) Adjust heat at table to maintain strong simmer throughout cooking. As each kind of food is cooked (3 to 5 minutes), diners are served or serve themselves from the cooking pot. (Discard any clams that do not open.) Add remaining ingredients from platter, about ¼ at a time, as needed. Add hot Dashi mixture or boiling water to pot to maintain satisfactory level of broth for cooking, if necessary.

10. For each person, place 3 tablespoons Ponzu Sauce in individual small bowls. As food is served, dip pieces into sauce mixed with choice of daikon or green onion. Pass any remaining Ponzu Sauce.

*Makes 5 to 6 servings*

*If desired, use only 2 or 3 of the seafood ingredients; increase proportionately the amounts of those selected.

**Appropriate utensils for table-cooking include Mongolian hot pot; cast-iron pot; earthenware pot or casserole; flameproof (not oven-proof) ceramic casserole; deep-sided electric skillet; chafing dish; or fondue pot. If utensil is not electric, a portable heat source, with adjustable heat, is needed. If necessary, use 2 utensils; divide broth and cook in both simultaneously. (If unavailable, cook on top of range and serve immediately.)

3                    3          7          9

# Seafood and Vegetable Saute

(Teppan-Yaki)

1¼ pounds boneless meat (beef, chicken, lamb, liver, pork)*
4 hard-shell clams
3 quarts water
4¼ teaspoons salt
8 large shrimp, in shells
8 medium fresh black Chinese mushrooms
4 small green bell peppers
2 leeks
1 or 2 medium yellow onions
1 large carrot, 1 to 1½ inches in diameter
2 small ears corn, husked
1 or 2 medium (white- or yellow-fleshed) sweet potatoes
2 small thin eggplants (about 3 ounces)
Sesame Seed Sauce (recipe follows)
Ponzu Sauce (see page 78)
6 tablespoons grated pared daikon, drained
3 tablespoons thinly sliced green onion
Seven-spice powder (Shichimi togarashi)
2 to 3 tablespoons prepared Japanese mustard
2 tablespoons vegetable oil

1. For easier slicing, freeze meat until firm but not frozen, 30 to 40 minutes.

2. Place clams in medium bowl with 1 quart water and 4 teaspoons salt; let stand 15 to 20 minutes. Rinse well under cold running water; drain.

3. Cut meat into ¹⁄₁₆- to ⅛-inch-thick slices. (If using chicken or liver, cut into 1½-inch squares.)

4. Shell shrimp, leaving tail and section of shell nearest tail attached. Remove vein by inserting wooden pick under vein and lifting gently.

5. Remove and discard stems from mushrooms. Cut green peppers lengthwise into halves or quarters. Cut leeks crosswise into 2-inch lengths. Cut yellow onions crosswise into ¼-inch-thick slices. Insert wooden pick horizontally through each onion slice to prevent rings from separating.

6. Cut carrot crosswise into ¼-inch-thick slices. Cut corn crosswise into 1½-inch lengths. Heat 1 quart water to boiling in 2-quart saucepan over high heat. Place carrot in sieve and lower into boiling water; cook 1 minute. Rinse under cold running water; drain. Add remaining ¼ teaspoon salt and the corn to boiling water. Reduce heat to medium; simmer 2 minutes. Drain.

7. Cut sweet potatoes crosswise into ¼-inch-thick slices; place in 2 cups water in medium bowl. Let stand 5 minutes; drain. Cut eggplants diagonally into ¼-inch-thick slices; place in remaining 2 cups water in medium bowl. Let stand 5 minutes; drain.

8. For dipping sauces: Prepare Sesame Seed Sauce in small bowl and ¼ cup Ponzu Sauce in second small bowl. As food is served, each person mixes sauces with choice of daikon, green onion, seven-spice powder and/or mustard.

9. Arrange meat, seafood and vegetables on platter.

10. At the table, heat oil in 10- or 12-inch skillet over medium-high heat.** Add about ¼ each of the meat, seafood and vegetables to skillet; cook, stirring and turning occasionally, until cooked to desired doneness, 4 to 6 minutes. (Discard any clams that do not open.) As each kind of food is cooked, diners are served or serve themselves from the skillet. Add remaining ingredients from platter, about ¼ at a time, as needed.

11. Dip hot, cooked pieces of food into sauce of choice. Pass remaining sauces as needed. *Makes 4 servings*

*Use 2 or 3 kinds of meat, dividing the 1¼-pounds total amount among them as desired.

**For cooking at the table, use electric skillet or use heavy skillet or griddle with portable heat source, such as a hot plate. If unavailable, cook on top of range and serve immediately.

## Sesame Seed Sauce
¾ cup white sesame seeds
1 tablespoon miso
1 tablespoon sugar
2 tablespoons mirin
2 tablespoons rice vinegar
2 tablespoons saké
6 tablespoons soy sauce
¾ teaspoon prepared Japanese mustard
1 to 4 tablespoons Dashi (optional) (see page 48)

1. Heat sesame seeds in 8- or 10-inch skillet over medium-high heat, stirring or shaking pan constantly, until seeds are light brown and first popping sound occurs. Grind seeds using mortar and pestle or grinder until smooth.

2. Place sesame seed paste in small bowl; stir in remaining ingredients, except Dashi. Mix well. If thinner sauce is preferred, stir in Dashi, 1 tablespoon at a time, until desired consistency is achieved. (Refrigerate, covered, any leftover sauce up to 2 days.)
*Makes about 1½ cups*

# VEGETABLES

# Vegetables in Spiced Coconut Milk
(Sayur Lodeh)

6 ounces boneless beef shoulder
    chuck
1 large carrot
4 ounces green beans, trimmed
4 ounces canned baby corn,
    drained
4 ounces cabbage
1 to 2 hot fresh green chili
    peppers, seeded
1 hot fresh red chili pepper,
    seeded
1 medium zucchini (about
    8 ounces), pared
2 cups water
1 ounce shallots, thinly sliced
2 cloves garlic, thinly sliced
1 piece (1×½ inch) fresh galingal
    or ¾ teaspoon ground laos
    powder
2 dried salam or curry leaves
1 teaspoon salt
1 cup Rich Coconut Milk (see page
    173)

1. Cut beef into 1×1×½-inch pieces. Cut carrot into ½-inch cubes. Cut green beans and baby corn crosswise into 1-inch pieces. Cut cabbage into 2-inch squares. Cut green and red chilies lengthwise into ⅛-inch strips. Cut zucchini lengthwise into ½-inch slices, then cut slices into 1-inch squares.

2. Heat water in large saucepan over high heat to boiling. Add beef. Reduce heat to low; simmer, covered, until beef is tender, about 30 minutes.

3. Add chilies, shallots, garlic, galingal, salam leaves and salt. Cook, uncovered, over medium heat, 5 minutes. Add carrot; cook, stirring occasionally, 5 minutes.

4. Add zucchini, corn, beans and cabbage. Decrease heat to medium-low; cook, uncovered, stirring occasionally, until vegetables are firm-tender, about 8 minutes. Stir in coconut milk. Reduce heat to low; cook, stirring constantly, 1 minute. Serve immediately. *Makes 6 servings*

1

4

4

# Asparagus in Oyster Sauce

1 pound fresh asparagus*
   Boiling water
2 tablespoons peanut oil
1 tablespoon minced green onion,
   white part only
2 teaspoons minced garlic
2 teaspoons minced pared fresh
   ginger root
2 tablespoons oyster sauce
2 tablespoons water

1. Snap off and discard tough woody ends of asparagus stalks. Arrange asparagus in steamer basket or steamer tray.

2. Place steamer basket on rack in wok. Add boiling water to wok to level of 1 inch below basket. Steam, covered, over medium heat, until asparagus is crisp-tender, about 7 minutes. Transfer asparagus to serving platter; keep warm, loosely covered.

3. Quickly prepare sauce. Wipe wok completely dry. Heat oil in wok over high heat until hot, about 30 seconds. Reduce heat to low; stir-fry onion, garlic and ginger until golden, about 30 seconds.

4. Add oyster sauce and 2 tablespoons water to wok. Increase heat to medium-high; cook and stir until sauce is slightly thickened, about 45 seconds. Pour sauce over asparagus. Serve immediately.     *Makes 3 to 4 servings*

*This recipe can be made with fresh broccoli in place of asparagus. Trim and pare stalks; cut lengthwise into ½-inch-thick pieces. Increase steaming time in Step 2 to 10 to 15 minutes.

# Stir-Fried Bean Sprouts

2 ounces salted fish fillet*
1½ ounces Chinese chives
½ cup peanut oil
4 cloves garlic, minced
1 pound fresh mung beans
    sprouts, rinsed and trimmed
1 or 2 hot fresh red chili peppers,
    seeded and finely slivered
1½ teaspoons soy sauce
1½ teaspoons rice wine
1½ teaspoons Chinese black vinegar
    or rice vinegar

1. Rinse fish thoroughly; pat dry. Cut fish crosswise into ¼-inch slices.

2. Trim and discard root ends from chives; cut chives crosswise into 1¼-inch pieces.

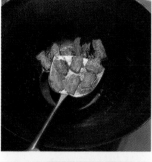

3. Heat oil in wok over high heat until hot, about 30 seconds. Add fish; stir-fry until crisp and flaky, 1 to 2 minutes. Remove with slotted spoon; drain on paper towels.

4. Remove and discard all but 3 table-spoons of oil from wok; heat over medium heat 15 seconds. Add garlic; stir-fry 10 seconds. Increase heat to high; add bean sprouts and chives and stir-fry 2 minutes. Reduce heat to medium; stir-fry 2 minutes.

5. Add chilies, soy sauce, rice wine and vinegar to wok; stir-fry 30 seconds. Transfer to serving dish; top with fish. Serve immediately.

*Makes 3 to 4 servings*

*If salted fish is not available, it can be omitted. Decrease oil to 3 tablespoons and add ½ teaspoon salt in Step 5.

# Hot and Spicy Shredded Cabbage

2 pounds napa cabbage (preferably near root end)
2 tablespoons salt
¼ cup water
1 piece pared fresh ginger root, 2x1¼x1¼ inches
1 to 3 dried red chili peppers
2 tablespoons sugar
2 tablespoons white vinegar
1 tablespoon soy sauce
3 tablespoons peanut oil
1 tablespoon sesame oil

1. Separate cabbage leaves; cut crosswise into 4-inch lengths. Stack a few leaves at a time and cut lengthwise into ³⁄₁₆-inch-wide shreds. Place cabbage in large bowl; sprinkle with salt and toss. Drizzle with water. Top cabbage with a plate and 3-pound weight, such as canned goods. Let stand 30 minutes.

2. Cut ginger lengthwise into ¹⁄₁₆-inch-thick slices; stack slices and cut lengthwise into ¹⁄₁₆-inch-wide shreds. Cut chili peppers crosswise with scissors into ⅛-inch pieces; remove and discard seeds.

3. Rinse cabbage thoroughly in large bowl of cold water, changing water several times; drain well. Squeeze cabbage between several layers of paper towels to remove excess water.

4. Combine cabbage, ginger and chili pepper in large bowl. Add sugar, vinegar and soy sauce; stir to mix well.

5. Heat wok over high heat 15 seconds. Add peanut and sesame oils and heat until hot, about 30 seconds. Add cabbage mixture; heat to boiling. Reduce heat to medium-low. Simmer, covered, stirring occasionally, just until cabbage is crisp-tender, about 5 minutes. Uncover wok; increase heat to high. Cook, stirring constantly and rapidly, 2 minutes. Serve hot, or refrigerate, covered, until cold; remove cabbage from liquid with slotted spoon and serve. *Makes 3 to 4 servings*

1

2

# Vegetarian Fried Vermicelli

9 medium dried black Chinese
    mushrooms
    Boiling water
5 ounces rice sticks
3 quarts warm water
1 large carrot
1 ounce dried sweet tofu strips
4 ounces fresh green beans,
    trimmed
5 tablespoons peanut oil
1½ teaspoons sugar
¼ teaspoon salt
4 ounces fresh mung bean sprouts,
    rinsed and trimmed
2 tablespoons soy sauce
2 or 3 fresh green chili peppers,
    sliced

1. Place mushrooms in bowl and cover with boiling water. Let soak 30 minutes. Drain mushrooms, straining and reserving ½ cup of the soaking liquid. Trim and discard stems; squeeze out excess water.

2. Place rice sticks in large bowl and cover with warm water. Let soak 20 minutes. Rinse under cold running water; drain well.

3. Cut mushrooms into ⅓-inch strips. Cut carrot crosswise into 1½-inch pieces; cut each piece lengthwise into ³⁄₁₆-inch slices, then cut each slice into ³⁄₁₆-inch strips. Cut tofu strips crosswise with scissors into ½-inch pieces. (If too fragile to cut, break strips into irregular pieces.) Diagonally cut green beans crosswise into ½-inch slices.

4. Heat 4 tablespoons of the oil in wok over high heat 30 seconds. Reduce heat to medium; add tofu strips. Stir-fry until evenly blistered, 20 to 30 seconds. Remove and drain on paper towels.

5. Add mushrooms to oil remaining in wok; stir-fry 30 seconds. Increase heat to high; add carrot and stir-fry 35 seconds. Add green beans; stir-fry 20 seconds. Sprinkle with sugar and salt; mix well. Transfer vegetables to plate.

6. Add remaining 1 tablespoon oil to wok; heat over medium heat until hot. Add bean sprouts and rice sticks; stir-fry 1 minute. Add reserved soaking liquid and the soy sauce. Cook and stir 1 minute. Return vegetables and tofu strips to wok; cook and stir 1 minute. Serve immediately with chili peppers.

*Makes 4 to 6 servings*

# Hot and Sour Cucumbers

1¼ pounds very thin cucumbers*
1 tablespoon salt
¼ cup plus 1½ tablespoons cold
    water
2 green onions, white part only
1 to 3 dried chili peppers, seeded
1 large clove garlic
1 tablespoon cornstarch
2 tablespoons chicken broth
2 tablespoons Chinese black
    vinegar
1 tablespoon soy sauce
1 tablespoon rice wine
1 tablespoon sugar
4 tablespoons peanut oil

1. Slant-cut cucumbers at ⅛-inch intervals, leaving slices attached ⅜ inch from bottom on first 3 cuts; cut through to detach piece on fourth cut. (If cucumbers are larger than 1¼ inches in diameter, cut pieces in half lengthwise.) Place cucumbers in medium bowl; sprinkle with salt and toss. Drizzle with ¼ cup water. Top cucumbers with a plate and 3-pound weight, such as canned goods; let stand 10 minutes.

2. Cut onions crosswise into ½-inch pieces. Cut chili peppers crosswise into ½-inch pieces. Pound garlic lightly with flat side of cleaver.

3. Mix cornstarch and 1½ tablespoons cold water until smooth; stir in chicken broth, vinegar, soy sauce, rice wine and sugar until sugar dissolves.

4. Rinse cucumbers thoroughly in sieve under cold running water; drain well. Pat dry between several layers of paper towels.

5. Heat wok over high heat 15 seconds; add 3 tablespoons oil and heat until hot, about 30 seconds. Reduce heat to low. Add chili pepper and garlic, stir-fry until pepper is dark red, about 10 seconds. Add onion; stir-fry 10 seconds. Increase heat to high. Scatter in cucumbers, ¼ at a time; stir-fry until crisp-tender, about 3 minutes after all cucumbers are added. Stir cornstarch mixture and add to wok; cook and stir until thickened, about 30 seconds. Drizzle with 1 tablespoon oil; stir 2 or 3 times. Discard garlic. Serve immediately.          *Makes 4 servings*

*Use long thin waxless cucumbers, about 1 inch in diameter, found in Oriental grocery stores. If unavailable, use seedless cucumbers.

# Spicy Eggplant

1 pound eggplant (preferably thin)
6 ounces boneless pork shoulder
8 to 10 green onions, white part
   only
2 tablespoons soy sauce
1½ tablespoons ground brown bean
   sauce
1 tablespoon rice wine
1 tablespoon Chinese black
   vinegar
1 tablespoon sugar
2 teaspoons chili sauce with
   soybean
4 cups vegetable oil
2 tablespoons peanut oil
2 teaspoons minced pared fresh
   ginger root
1 clove garlic, minced

1. Pare ½-inch-wide strips of skin lengthwise at ½-inch intervals around eggplant. Cut eggplant lengthwise into 1-inch-wide wedges; cut wedges into 3-inch lengths. Place eggplant in bowl with cold water to cover.

2. Cut pork across the grain into ⅛-inch-thick slices; cut slices into 2×1-inch pieces. Cut onions into 1½-inch lengths.

3. Mix soy sauce, bean sauce, rice wine, vinegar, sugar and chili sauce in small bowl.

4. Heat wok over high heat 20 seconds; add vegetable oil and heat to 375°F. Drain eggplant; pat dry with paper towels. Fry eggplant, ½ at a time, until golden and just barely tender, 1½ to 2 minutes. Remove eggplant with strainer; drain on paper towels. Gently blot with more paper towels. Remove oil from wok; wipe clean.

5. Heat wok over high heat 15 seconds; add peanut oil and heat until hot, about 30 seconds. Stir-fry onions 1 minute; remove with slotted spoon to plate.

6. Stir-fry pork in oil remaining in wok 1 minute. Push pork to side; reduce heat to medium. Stir-fry ginger and garlic 10 seconds; then mix in pork. Increase heat to high. Stir in soy sauce mixture. Return onions to wok. Cook and stir until sauce thickens slightly, about 1 minute. Stir in eggplant; stir and toss until coated with sauce and heated through, about 30 seconds. *Makes 3 to 4 servings*

1

4

6

1

6

7

# Miso Eggplant
(Nasu Miso-Itame)

3 small thin eggplants (about 4 ounces each)
2½ cups water
3 small green bell peppers
1 cube (½ inch) pared fresh ginger root
2 tablespoons miso
1 tablespoon soy sauce
1 tablespoon sugar
1 teaspoon cornstarch
1½ tablespoons cold water
3 tablespoons vegetable oil
4 ounces ground pork or chicken
1 tablespoon saké

1. Cut each eggplant crosswise into 2-inch lengths; cut lengthwise into 1-inch-thick wedges. Make 2 or 3 shallow cuts in skin of each wedge. Immediately place eggplant in 2 cups water; let stand 5 minutes. Drain; pat dry with paper towels. Cut each green pepper in half lengthwise; cut halves into 1×2-inch pieces. Mince ginger.

2. Mix remaining ½ cup water, the miso, soy sauce and sugar in small bowl. Stir until sugar dissolves; reserve.

3. Mix cornstarch and 1½ tablespoons cold water in small bowl until smooth; reserve.

4. Heat wok or 10-inch skillet over high heat 30 seconds; add oil and heat until hot. Add pork; cook, stirring constantly, until pork turns white, about 2 minutes.

5. Add ginger, eggplant and green pepper to wok; cook, stirring constantly, until vegetables are almost tender, 3 to 4 minutes.

6. Add saké to wok; cook 30 seconds. Stir in miso mixture.

7. Stir cornstarch mixture; add to wok. Cook and stir until sauce thickens, about 1 minute. Serve immediately.
*Makes 4 to 5 servings*

# Lemon Sweet Potatoes

(Satsuma-Imo Amani)

**1 pound sweet potatoes (preferably long and thin)\***
**Water**
**1 medium lemon**
**3 tablespoons sugar**
**⅛ teaspoon salt**

1. Pare sweet potatoes; remove any dark spots. Cut potatoes crosswise into 1-inch-thick slices. Place in medium bowl with water to cover. Soak 10 minutes. Change water twice during soaking time. Drain.

2. Cut lemon crosswise into ⅛-inch-thick slices.

3. Place potatoes, 2½ cups water, the sugar and salt in 2-quart saucepan; heat to boiling over high heat. Reduce heat to medium; boil gently 10 minutes. Add lemon slices. Continue cooking, adding more water if necessary, until potatoes are tender, about 20 minutes longer. Drain; place in serving bowl. Serve hot, or cool to room temperature.     *Makes 4 servings*

\*White- or yellow-fleshed sweet potatoes can be used. If using light-colored potatoes, you may wish to add a few drops yellow food coloring when adding the lemon slices.

# Flavored Vegetables with Chicken

(Chikuzen-Ni)

4 medium dried black Chinese
    mushrooms
  Boiling water
6 ounces carrots (about
    3 medium)
1 ounce snow peas
3 cups cold water
1 teaspoon vinegar
6 ounces burdock root
4 ounces lotus root, pared
10 ounces boneless chicken
    (skinned, if desired)
½ teaspoon salt
  Water
2 tablespoons sugar
3 tablespoons soy sauce
1 tablespoon mirin

1. Soak mushrooms in boiling water until tender, 20 to 30 minutes; drain mushrooms, reserving 1½ cups of the soaking liquid. Remove and discard stems from mushrooms.

2. Cut carrots into 1-inch irregularly shaped pieces. Cut off ends of snow peas; remove strings.

3. Place cold water and vinegar in medium bowl. Scrape brown skin off burdock root with back of knife; cut into 1-inch irregularly shaped pieces. Immediately place burdock root into cold-water mixture.

4. Cut lotus root crosswise into ¼-inch-thick slices. Immediately add lotus root to cold-water mixture. Let stand 5 minutes. Drain burdock and lotus root. Cut chicken into 1-inch-square pieces.

5. Place mushrooms, carrots, burdock root, lotus root, chicken and salt in 3-quart saucepan; add water to cover. Heat to boiling over high heat; add snow peas. Boil 30 seconds. Immedi-

ately remove from heat; drain. Rinse under cold running water; drain. Remove and reserve snow peas.

6. Place reserved mushroom soaking liquid and sugar in 3-quart saucepan; add chicken mixture. Cover saucepan; heat to boiling over high heat. Reduce heat to medium; boil gently, covered, 15 minutes, stirring occasionally.

7. Add soy sauce and mirin. Continue cooking, covered, until chicken is cooked through and vegetables are tender, about 3 minutes. Add snow peas; cook 2 minutes longer. Serve hot, or cool to room temperature.

*Makes 4 servings*

Note: This dish may be prepared up to 2 days in advance of serving. Refrigerate, covered. Allow to come to room temperature.

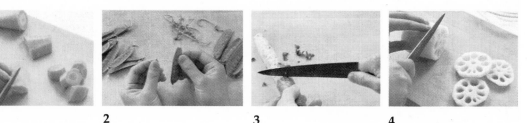

1      2      2      3      4

# Japanese Pumpkin

(Kabocha Nimono)

1 pound Japanese pumpkin or
    green winter squash (such as
    acorn)
1½ to 2 cups Dashi (see page 48)
2½ tablespoons sugar
1 tablespoon mirin
1½ tablespoons soy sauce

1. Cut pumpkin in half; remove seeds. Wash pumpkin. Cut into pieces approximately 2-inches square.

2. Slice off small pieces (about ½ inch) of pumpkin skin, to give surface a mottled appearance. (Pare skin completely, if desired.)

3. Place pumpkin, skin side down, in heavy, 3-quart saucepan. Add 1½ cups Dashi, the sugar and mirin.

4. Cut parchment paper or aluminum foil to fit into saucepan; lay loosely on top of pumpkin. Cover saucepan securely with lid.

5. Heat to boiling over medium heat. Boil vigorously 4 minutes; gently turn pumpkin pieces over. Continue boiling, covered with paper and lid, 4 minutes longer.

6. Add soy sauce. Add remaining ½ cup Dashi, if needed. Continue boiling, covered with paper and lid, 7 to 8 minutes longer, just until tender. Serve hot, or cool to room temperature.

*Makes 4 servings*

1

2

3

# Curried Yellow Peas with Potato

(Chana Dal with Potato)

1½ cups (about 9 ounces) chana dal (dried Indian yellow split peas)*

2½ quarts water

1 large potato (about 9 ounces), pared

1½ ounces shallots, chopped

1 piece (2×1 inches) pared fresh ginger root, chopped

3 cloves garlic, chopped

1 or 2 long thin fresh green chili peppers

3 tablespoons vegetable oil

1 medium onion, chopped

1 teaspoon ground turmeric

2 teaspoons black mustard seeds

3 whole cardamom pods

1 piece (1 inch) cinnamon stick

⅓ cup fresh coriander leaves, coarsely chopped

1½ teaspoons salt

Indian flat bread, such as chapati, poori or naan (optional)

1. Sort through peas, discarding any small stones, debris and discolored peas. Rinse thoroughly under cold running water. Place peas and 1 quart of the water in medium bowl; let soak 30 minutes.

2. Cut potato into ½-inch cubes. Combine shallots, ginger and garlic in mortar with pestle until coarsely ground. Cut chili lengthwise into ⅛-inch strips; discard seeds.

3. Drain peas; combine with 3 cups of the water in large saucepan. Heat over high heat to boiling. Reduce heat to medium; cook, uncovered, stirring frequently, 15 minutes. Drain peas.

4. Heat oil in large saucepan over medium heat until hot, about 30 seconds. Add onion and shallot mixture; cook and stir until onion is golden, about 5 minutes. Stir in turmeric.

5. Add 3 cups of the water; heat to boiling. Reduce heat to low; simmer, uncovered, 5 minutes. Add potato; cook 7 minutes. Stir in mustard seeds, cardamom and cinnamon.

6. Add peas, chili pepper, coriander and salt; mix well. Heat over high heat to boiling. Reduce heat to low; simmer, covered, stirring occasionally, until peas are tender, 15 to 20 minutes. Remove and discard cardamom and cinnamon. Serve with Indian bread.

*Makes 6 to 8 servings*

*Available in Indian grocery stores.

# Vegetable Stir-Fry

2 ounces Chinese pickled cabbage
½ cup shelled fresh peas or thawed
  frozen peas
  Boiling water
3 medium green bell peppers
1 ounce canned bamboo shoots,
  rinsed and drained
3 tablespoons peanut oil
2 tablespoons finely chopped
  green onion, white part only
1 teaspoon minced pared fresh
  ginger root
1 tablespoon soy sauce
1 tablespoon rice wine
1 teaspoon sugar

1. Soak cabbage in bowl of cold water
10 minutes; drain well. If not already
shredded, cut cabbage into ⅛-inch-
wide shreds. Squeeze dry between paper towels.

2. If using fresh peas, add to small
saucepan of boiling water; cook 1
minute. Rinse under cold water to
cool; drain well.

3. Cut green peppers lengthwise into
³⁄₁₆-inch-wide strips. Cut bamboo
shoots lengthwise into ⅛-inch-thick
slices. Stack slices and cut lengthwise
into ¹⁄₁₆-inch-wide shreds; cut shreds
crosswise into 1½-inch lengths.

4. Heat wok over high heat 15 seconds; add oil and heat until hot, about
30 seconds. Reduce heat to medium.
Add onion and ginger; stir-fry 10 seconds. Increase heat to high. Add bamboo shoots; stir-fry 30 seconds. Add
cabbage; stir-fry 30 seconds. Scatter in
peppers, ⅓ at a time; stir-fry 2 minutes
after all peppers are added. Add peas;
stir-fry 30 seconds. Add soy sauce, rice
wine and sugar. Cook and stir 15 seconds. Serve immediately.

*Makes 3 to 4 servings*

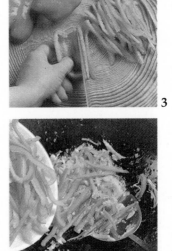

# Buddha's Delight

1 ounce small dried black Chinese
    mushrooms (about 14)
4 cups boiling water
¼ ounce dried cloud ears
1 ounce dried lily buds
3 cups warm water
1 ounce dried cellophane noodles
1½ quarts hot water
6 ounces green cabbage
2 large carrots
1 ounce dried sweet bean curd
    strips
5 tablespoons peanut oil
1 cube preserved red bean curd
    plus 1 teaspoon liquid
1 tablespoon soy sauce
1 tablespoon sugar
1 to 2 teaspoons sesame oil
    (optional)

1. Place black Chinese mushrooms and 2 cups boiling water in small bowl. Place cloud ears and remaining 2 cups boiling water in another small bowl. Place lily buds and 3 cups warm water in third bowl. Let mushrooms, cloud ears and lily buds soak 30 minutes. Combine noodles and hot water in medium bowl. Let soak 10 minutes.

2. Drain noodles; cut into 5-inch lengths.

3. Drain mushrooms, straining and reserving 1 cup of the soaking liquid. Trim and discard stems; squeeze out excess water.

4. Drain cloud ears; rinse under cold running water; pat dry. Pinch off and discard hard tough "eye" at base of petals.

5. Drain lily buds; rinse under cold running water; squeeze out excess water. Pinch off and discard knobby end; tie each bud into a knot.

6. Cut cabbage into 2½×2-inch pieces. Diagonally cut carrots crosswise into ⅛-inch slices. Cut bean curd strips crosswise into 1-inch-wide pieces. (If too fragile to cut, break strips into irregular pieces.)

7. Heat peanut oil in wok over high heat until hot, about 30 seconds. Reduce heat to medium; add red bean curd and liquid. Stir-fry, mashing with back of spoon, 45 seconds. Add bean curd strips; stir-fry until evenly blistered, 20 to 30 seconds.

8. Increase heat to high. Add cabbage and carrots; stir-fry 2 minutes. Stir in mushrooms, cloud ears, lily buds and noodles. Add reserved soaking liquid, the soy sauce and sugar; mix well. Heat to boiling. Reduce heat to low; simmer, covered, stirring occasionally to prevent sticking, until most of the liquid has been absorbed, 10 to 12 minutes. Drizzle with sesame oil; stir 2 or 3 times. Serve immediately.

*Makes 4 servings*

1

5

6

7

# RICE & NOODLES

## Cellophane Noodles with Beef and Vegetables

(Chap Chae)

½ **pound boneless beef sirloin or
   top round steak**
6 **medium dried black Chinese
   mushrooms**
   **Boiling water**
1½ **tablespoons sesame seeds**
3 **tablespoons soy sauce**
1½ **tablespoons sugar**
1 **tablespoon sesame oil**
2 to 4 **cloves garlic, crushed
   through press**
¼ **teaspoon ground black pepper**
2 **large mild fresh green chili
   peppers or 1 medium green
   bell pepper, seeded**
1 **medium onion**
1 **large carrot**
4 **quarts water**
½ **pound fresh spinach, washed,
   well drained**
2 **ounces cellophane noodles (bean
   threads)**
1 **large egg, separated**
4 **tablespoons vegetable oil**
⅛ to ¼ **teaspoon salt**

1. For easier slicing, freeze beef until firm but not frozen, 30 to 40 minutes.

2. Place mushrooms in bowl and cover with boiling water. Let soak 30 minutes. Drain. Trim and remove stems; squeeze out excess water.

3. Toast sesame seeds in small dry skillet over medium heat, stirring constantly, until golden, about 5 minutes; transfer to plate and let cool. Pound seeds in mortar with pestle until partially ground (about half the seeds should be powdery).

4. Cut meat across the grain into ⅛-inch slices, then cut slices into ⅛-inch strips. Combine 2 tablespoons of the soy sauce, 1 tablespoon of the sugar, 1 tablespoon of the sesame seeds, ½ tablespoon of the sesame oil, the garlic and black pepper in medium bowl; stir until sugar dissolves. Add beef; mix well. Let marinate at least 15 minutes.

5. Cut mushrooms into ¹⁄₁₆-inch strips. Cut chili peppers into 2×⅛-inch pieces. Cut onion in half lengthwise; cut halves into ⅛-inch slices. Cut carrot into 1½×⅛×¹⁄₁₆-inch pieces.

6. Heat 2 quarts of the water in large saucepan over high heat to boiling. Add spinach; cook just until limp and bright green, 20 to 30 seconds. Drain and rinse under cold running water. Squeeze spinach to remove as much water as possible; cut in half crosswise.

7. Heat remaining 2 quarts water in large saucepan over high heat to boiling. Add noodles. Reduce heat to medium; cook just until noodles are limp and rubbery, 30 to 45 seconds. Rinse under cold running water; drain well. Cut noodles with scissors into 3-inch pieces.

8. Lightly beat egg white and yolk in separate bowls. Heat lightly oiled small skillet over low heat 1 minute. Add egg white, tilting pan to form even layer. Cook until completely set, 1 to 2 minutes; transfer to plate. Repeat with egg yolk. Roll up egg white and egg yolk sheets; cut crosswise into thin shreds.

9. Heat ½ tablespoon of the vegetable oil in medium skillet over medium heat until hot, about 20 seconds. Add onion; cook and stir until soft, 3 to 4 minutes. Sprinkle with a pinch of salt; mix and transfer to large bowl. Using ½ tablespoon vegetable oil and a pinch of salt for each vegetable, repeat procedure, cooking chili peppers 2 to 3 minutes, carrot 3 to 4 minutes, mushrooms 3 minutes and spinach 3 minutes.

10. Heat ½ tablespoon of the vegetable oil in skillet over medium heat until hot, about 20 seconds. Add beef; cook and stir until beef is no longer red and juices have evaporated, about 5 minutes; transfer to bowl.

11. Combine remaining 1 tablespoon soy sauce, ½ tablespoon sesame seeds, ½ tablespoon sugar and ½ tablespoon sesame oil in small bowl; stir until sugar is dissolved. Heat remaining 1 tablespoon vegetable oil in skillet over medium heat. Add noodles; cook and stir 15 seconds. Stir in soy sauce mixture; cook and stir just until noodles are evenly colored, 20 to 30 seconds.

12. Quickly add beef and vegetables to skillet; cook and stir just until well mixed and hot, about 30 seconds. Transfer to serving dish; garnish with egg shreds. Serve immediately.

*Makes 3 to 4 servings*

5                                      7

# Dry Beef Noodle

(Bun Thit)

¾ **pound boneless beef sirloin steak**

4 **ounces fresh mung bean sprouts, rinsed and trimmed**

1 **quart boiling water**

1 **small cucumber (about 5 ounces), pared**

1½ **cups coarsely shredded romaine lettuce**

1½ **quarts plus 1 cup water**

½ **cup nuoc mam (fish sauce)**

¼ **cup fresh lime juice**

¼ **cup sugar**

1 **clove garlic, minced**

6 **ounces rice sticks**

⅓ **cup roasted unsalted peanuts**

1½ **tablespoons chopped fresh coriander leaves**

1½ **tablespoons chopped green onion, tops only**

1½ **tablespoons chopped fresh mint leaves**

2 **long thin fresh red chili peppers, seeded, thinly sliced**

1 **large onion**

1½ **teaspoons sugar**

¼ **teaspoon salt**

⅛ **teaspoon ground black pepper**

3 **tablespoons vegetable oil**

2 **cloves garlic, very thinly sliced**

1. For easier slicing, freeze beef until firm but not frozen, 30 to 40 minutes.

2. Place bean sprouts in sieve; pour 1 quart boiling water over sprouts to blanch. Rinse briefly under cold running water; drain well.

3. Cut cucumber crosswise into ³⁄₁₆-inch slices, then cut each slice into ³⁄₁₆-inch strips. Arrange cucumber, sprouts and lettuce on large serving platter, leaving room for noodles. Refrigerate, covered.

4. For sauce, combine 1 cup of the water, the nuoc mam, lime juice, sugar and minced garlic in small bowl; stir until sugar is dissolved.

5. Cut beef across the grain into ¹⁄₁₆-inch slices, then cut slices into 2×½-inch pieces. Reserve at room temperature.

6. Heat remaining 1½ quarts water in large saucepan over high heat to boiling. Add rice sticks. Reduce heat to medium; cook, stirring occasionally, 5 minutes. Drain noodles; rinse briefly under cold running water. Drain well; reserve, covered, at room tempera-

ture. Before serving, put noodles on plate with cucumber, sprouts and lettuce.

7. Chop peanuts; crush slightly in mortar with pestle or on board with rolling pin. Mix coriander, green onion tops and mint in small bowl. Arrange peanuts, mixed herbs and chili peppers on small plate.

8. Cut onion in half lengthwise, then cut crosswise into ⅛-inch slices. Mix sugar, salt and black pepper in small cup.

9. Heat oil in medium skillet over high heat until hot. Add onion and sliced garlic. Reduce heat to medium; cook and stir until brown, 8 to 10 minutes. Stir-fry beef, adding ¼ at a time, just until beef is slightly pink, about 4 minutes. Add sugar mixture; mix well and remove from heat.

10. To serve, divide lettuce, cucumber and bean sprouts among 4 wide shallow soup bowls. Top each serving with ¼ of the noodles, then with ¼ of the hot beef mixture. Serve with peanuts, mixed herbs, chili peppers and sauce. Add condiments according to individual tastes. *Makes 4 servings*

# Noodles with Meat and Gravy

(Mee Rebus)

1 pound boneless lamb shoulder
    or beef round roast
7 quarts plus 2¼ cups water
2 stalks fresh lemon grass
4 ounces shallots
4 to 6 cloves garlic
1 ounce fresh galingal or
    1 teaspoon ground laos
    powder
2 to 4 tablespoons Malaysian curry
    powder
½ cup preserved whole brown
    soybeans, drained
½ cup vegetable oil
1 cup mashed cooked sweet
    potatoes
⅓ cup roasted unsalted peanuts,
    coarsely ground
4 small tomatoes, cut into halves
1 tablespoon sugar
6 ounces fried pressed tofu, diced
3 or 4 hard-cooked eggs, cut into
    wedges
4 to 6 small limes, halved
4 to 6 hot fresh red and green chili
    peppers, seeded, thinly sliced
½ cup Chinese celery leaves,
    chopped* (optional)
½ cup chopped green onions
½ cup Fried Onion Flakes (see page
    35)
1 pound fresh or thawed frozen
    yellow wheat noodles
¾ pound fresh mung bean sprouts,
    rinsed and trimmed

1. Cut meat into ½-inch cubes; combine with 3 cups of the water in medium saucepan. Heat over high heat to boiling. Reduce heat to low; simmer, covered, until meat is tender, about 25 minutes. Reserve meat and cooking liquid.

2. Trim root ends of lemon grass. Cut off tapering upper green leaf portion, leaving about 5-inch-long bulbous stalk. Peel off tough outer layers of bulbous stalk. Discard all trimmings. Cut stalks into thin slices.

3. Process lemon grass, shallots, garlic, galingal and curry powder in food processor or blender to a smooth paste; add up to ¼ cup of water if necessary to aid processing.

4. Mash soybeans with fork in small bowl to a smooth paste.

5. Heat oil in Dutch oven over high heat until hot, about 45 seconds. Reduce heat to medium; add shallot paste and stir-fry 10 minutes. Add 3 cups water, the soybean paste and sweet potatoes; mix well. Add reserved meat and cooking liquid and peanuts; mix well. Heat to boiling. Reduce heat to medium-low; cook, uncovered, stirring occasionally, 20 minutes. Stir in tomatoes and sugar; keep warm, covered, over very low heat while completing recipe.

6. Arrange accompaniments (tofu, eggs, limes, chili peppers, celery leaves, green onions and Fried Onion Flakes) on large serving platter.

7. Heat 4 quarts of the water in large saucepan over high heat to boiling. Add noodles. Reduce heat to medium; cook just until noodles are firm-tender, about 2 minutes. Drain well. Heat remaining 2 quarts water in large saucepan over high heat to boiling. Add bean sprouts; cook 10 seconds. Drain well. Arrange noodles and bean sprouts on second serving platter.

8. To serve, place noodles and sprouts in bottom of large individual bowls; ladle meat-gravy mixture over noodles. Add accompaniments according to individual tastes.

*Makes 6 servings*

*Available in Oriental grocery stores.

# Simmered Noodle Casserole

(Nabeyaki Udon)

2½ quarts water
14 ounces dried udon noodles
3 cups cold water
8 ounces boneless skinless chicken
6 tablespoons plus 1 teaspoon soy sauce
1 tablespoon saké
¾ teaspoon salt
4 ounces fresh spinach, washed, well drained
4 to 6 large green onions
1 medium carrot
4 medium or 8 to 12 small fresh black Chinese mushrooms
5⅔ cups Dashi (see page 48)
½ teaspoon sugar
3 tablespoons mirin
4 large eggs
    Seven-spice powder (shichimi togarashi)

1. Heat 2 quarts water to boiling in large kettle over high heat. Add noodles, a few at a time, stirring gently to separate. When water returns to full rolling boil, add 1 cup cold water; repeat 2 more times, using remaining cold water. When water returns to boiling, check for doneness; cook noodles until firm-tender (do not overcook).* Drain in sieve or colander; rinse under cold running water. Drain; cover with damp kitchen towel.

2. Cut chicken into 1-inch squares. Place chicken in small bowl; sprinkle with 1 tablespoon soy sauce and the saké. Let stand 10 minutes; drain.

3. Place remaining 2 cups water, ¼ teaspoon salt and the spinach in 2-quart saucepan; heat to boiling over high heat. Reduce heat to medium; simmer 2 minutes. Rinse under cold running water; drain. Squeeze spinach gently to remove excess moisture. Cut into 1-inch lengths.

4. Cut green onions into 1½-inch lengths. Cut carrot crosswise into ⅛-inch-thick slices; if desired, cut slices into halves or quarters. Remove and discard stems from mushrooms; if desired, mark shallow, V-shaped cuts in crisscross design on cap of each mushroom.

5. Place ⅔ cup Dashi, 1 teaspoon soy sauce, the sugar and carrot in 2-quart saucepan; heat to boiling over medium-high heat. Boil carrot gently 2 minutes. Add chicken; boil gently 2 minutes. Add mushrooms; boil gently 1 minute. Drain.

6. Place remaining 5 cups Dashi, 5 tablespoons soy sauce and ½ teaspoon salt and the mirin in 2-quart saucepan; heat to boiling over medium-high heat. Reduce heat to low to maintain low simmer until ready to add broth to casseroles.

7. Place noodles in 4 individual (3- to 4-cup size) flameproof earthenware casseroles,** dividing evenly; top with carrot, chicken and mushrooms. Add broth to a level even with top of noodles; cover each casserole. Heat to boiling over medium heat. Add spinach and green onions; break 1 egg onto center of ingredients in each casserole. Reduce heat to low; simmer, covered, until egg whites are just set. Serve immediately; pass seven-spice powder. *Makes 4 servings*

*Cooking time depends upon thickness and content of noodles; follow individual package directions for proper cooking time. (If desired, omit cold water and cook noodles at full rolling boil until firm-tender, 7 to 11 minutes.)

**Flameproof ceramic casseroles or even small, heavy ceramic saucepans may be used. If individual containers are not available, prepare in 1 large container.

1

1

4

7

7

# Bean Threads with Minced Pork

4 ounces cellophane noodles (bean threads)
32 dried black Chinese mushrooms
Hot water
1 small hot fresh red or green chili pepper
3 green onions
2 tablespoons minced fresh ginger root
2 tablespoons hot bean sauce
1½ cups chicken broth
1 tablespoon soy sauce
1 tablespoon dry sherry
2 tablespoons vegetable oil
6 ounces lean ground pork
2 fresh coriander sprigs

1. Place bean threads and dried mushrooms in separate bowls. Cover each with hot water. Let soak 30 minutes; drain. Cut bean threads into 4-inch pieces. Trim and discard mushroom stems; squeeze out excess water. Cut caps into thin slices.

2. Cut chili pepper in half and scrape out seeds. Finely mince chili pepper. Thinly slice 2 of the green onions. Cut remaining onion into 1½-inch slivers. Combine ginger and hot bean sauce in small bowl. Combine chicken broth, soy sauce and sherry in medium bowl.

3. Heat oil in wok or large skillet over high heat until hot. Add pork; cook and stir, breaking pork into small pieces, until it is no longer pink, about 2 minutes. Add chili pepper, sliced onions and ginger-bean sauce mixture. Stir-fry until meat absorbs color from bean sauce, about 1 minute.

4. Add chicken broth mixture, bean threads and mushrooms. Reduce heat to low; simmer, uncovered, until most of the liquid is absorbed, about 5 minutes. Garnish with onion slivers and coriander sprigs.

*Makes 4 servings*

1

2

# Stir-Fried Noodles with Pork and Shrimp

3 quarts plus 2 cups water
¾ pound boneless pork shoulder butt
¾ pound medium shrimp, shelled, deveined, tails intact
   Ice water
2 large eggs
6 tablespoons peanut oil
¾ pound fresh Chinese egg noodles
2 tablespoons soy sauce
1 tablespoon rice wine
½ teaspoon sugar
2 tablespoons minced pared fresh ginger root
2 cloves garlic, minced
½ pound fresh mung bean sprouts, rinsed and trimmed
⅓ cup Chinese chives, cut into 2-inch pieces

1. Heat 2 cups of the water in small saucepan over high heat to boiling. Add pork. Reduce heat to medium-low; cook, covered, 25 minutes. Add shrimp; cook, covered, 3 minutes. Drain pork and shrimp, reserving 1 cup of the cooking broth. Immediately plunge pork and shrimp into ice water.

2. Combine eggs and 1 tablespoon oil in medium bowl; beat thoroughly but lightly, creating as few bubbles as possible. Heat 8- or 9-inch nonstick skillet or heavy well-seasoned skillet over low heat 1 minute; brush lightly with some of the oil. Add ½ of the egg mixture, rotating skillet to spread evenly. Cook until egg is set, about 1 minute. Transfer egg pancake to plate or board. Repeat with remaining egg mixture.

3. When egg pancakes are cool, roll up into cylinders; cut crosswise into ⅛-inch slices. Unroll into individual strands; reserve, loosely covered.

4. Heat remaining 3 quarts water in large saucepan over high heat to boiling. Add noodles. Reduce heat to medium; cook just until firm-tender, 2 to 3 minutes. Drain; immediately rinse under cold running water until cool. Drain well.

5. Drain pork and shrimp well. Trim fat from pork. Cut pork across the grain into ¼-inch slices, then cut slices into 1½×½-inch pieces.

6. Mix reserved broth, soy sauce, rice wine and sugar in small bowl.

7. Heat 2 tablespoons of the oil in wok over high heat until hot, about 30 seconds. Stir-fry pork 1½ minutes; remove with slotted spoon.

8. Add remaining oil to wok; heat until hot. Reduce heat to low; stir-fry ginger and garlic 10 seconds. Increase heat to high; stir-fry bean sprouts 30 seconds. Reduce heat to medium. Stir-fry noodles, adding ⅓ at a time. Continue stir-frying 2 minutes after all are added.

9. Increase heat to high; add pork, shrimp and chives to wok. Stir-fry until heated, about 1 minute. Add broth mixture; cook and stir until most of the liquid has been absorbed but mixture is still moist.

10. Transfer mixture to serving dish; garnish with egg strands. Serve immediately. *Makes 4 servings*

# Chilled Summer Noodles

(Hyashi Somen)

**Dipping Sauce**
**1¼ cups Dashi (see page 48)**
   **6 tablespoons mirin**
   **6 tablespoons soy sauce**

**2½ quarts water**
  **12 to 14 ounces dried somen**
     **noodles**
   **2 cups cold water**
  **12 medium or 8 large shrimp, in**
     **shells**
   **¼ teaspoon salt**
   **2 small tomatoes**
   **1 long thin cucumber (preferably**
     **unwaxed)**
   **2 green onions**
   **1 quart ice water**
   **8 to 12 ice cubes**
   **2 tablespoons grated pared fresh**
     **ginger root**

1. For dipping sauce, heat Dashi, mirin and soy sauce to boiling in 1-quart saucepan. Cool completely. Refrigerate dipping sauce, covered, until cold.

2. Heat 2 quarts water to boiling in large kettle over high heat. Add noodles, a few at a time, stirring gently to separate. When water returns to full rolling boil, add 1 cup cold water; repeat, using remaining cold water. When water returns to full boil, check for doneness; cook noodles until firm-tender (do not overcook).* Drain in colander; rinse well and cool under cold running water. Drain; cover with damp kitchen towel. Cool completely.

3. Shell each shrimp, leaving tail and section of shell nearest tail attached. Remove veins. Heat remaining 2 cups water and the salt to boiling in 2-quart saucepan over high heat; add shrimp. When water returns to boiling, reduce heat to medium; simmer until shrimp are opaque and firm, 2 to 3 minutes. Drain; cool completely.

4. Cut each tomato lengthwise into 6 wedges. Cut cucumber diagonally into ⅛-inch-thick slices. Cut green onions into ⅛-inch-thick slices.

5. Place noodles in 4 medium serving bowls, dividing evenly; add ice water to a level even with top of noodles. Add 2 or 3 ice cubes to each bowl. Top each serving with shrimp, tomato and cucumber. Place ¼ cup dipping sauce in each of 4 small serving bowls. Dip noodles, shrimp and vegetables in sauce mixed with choice of green onion and/or ginger. Pass remaining dipping sauce.   *Makes 4 servings*

*Cooking time depends upon thickness and content of noodles; follow individual package directions for proper cooking time. (If desired, omit cold water and cook noodles at full rolling boil until firm-tender, 4 to 5 minutes.)

2

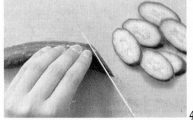

4

4

# Lo Mein Noodles with Shrimp

12 ounces Chinese-style thin egg
    noodles
 2 teaspoons sesame oil
1½ tablespoons oyster sauce
1½ tablespoons soy sauce
 ½ teaspoon sugar
 ¼ teaspoon salt
 ¼ teaspoon ground white pepper
 2 tablespoons vegetable oil
 1 teaspoon minced fresh ginger
    root
 1 clove garlic, minced
 8 ounces medium shrimp, shelled
    and deveined
 1 tablespoon dry sherry
 ½ cup Chinese chives cut into
    1-inch pieces or ¼ cup
    domestic chives cut into 1-inch
    pieces and 2 green onions cut
    into 1-inch pieces
 8 ounces fresh mung bean sprouts,
    rinsed and trimmed

1. Cook noodles according to package directions until firm-tender, 2 to 3 minutes. Drain, rinse under cold running water and drain again. Toss noodles with sesame oil until well coated.

2. Combine oyster sauce, soy sauce, sugar, salt and pepper in small bowl.

3. Heat vegetable oil in wok or large skillet over high heat. Add ginger and garlic and stir-fry 10 seconds. Add shrimp; stir-fry until shrimp begins to turn pink, about 1 minute. Add sherry and chives; stir-fry until chives begin to wilt, about 15 seconds. Add ½ of bean sprouts; stir-fry 15 seconds. Add remaining bean sprouts; stir-fry 15 seconds more.

4. Add oyster sauce mixture and noodles. Cook and stir until heated through, about 2 minutes.

*Makes 4 servings*

1

4

# Cashew Curry
(Kadju Sinhalese)

2 cups raw cashews (about
    9 ounces)
1 quart warm water
1 cup Rich Coconut Milk* (recipe
    follows)

**Curry Powder**
1 teaspoon ground coriander
1 teaspoon ground cumin
½ teaspoon ground fennel seeds
½ teaspoon ground turmeric
¼ teaspoon ground cinnamon
¼ teaspoon ground cardamom

2 tablespoons vegetable oil
1 medium onion, chopped
1 long thin fresh red chili pepper,
    seeded and finely chopped
6 dried curry leaves
1 teaspoon salt
½ teaspoon fenugreek seeds
½ teaspoon ground turmeric
    Dash ground red pepper
3 cups hot cooked rice

1. Rinse cashews well under cold running water; drain. Place cashews and warm water in medium bowl. Let soak 2 hours.

2. Prepare Rich Coconut Milk.

3. Combine Curry Powder ingredients in small bowl; mix well.

4. Drain cashews. Rinse and drain well.

5. Heat oil in medium saucepan over medium heat until hot, about 30 seconds. Add onion; cook and stir until onion is soft, about 4 minutes. Add chili, curry leaves, salt, fenugreek, turmeric, ground red pepper and 1 tablespoon of the Curry Powder; mix well.

6. Add cashews; stir in Rich Coconut Milk. Heat over medium heat to boiling. Reduce heat to low; simmer, covered, stirring occasionally, 10 minutes. Remove from heat; stir in remaining Curry Powder. Serve with rice.
*Makes 4 to 6 servings.*

*Unsweetened canned coconut milk can be substituted.

## Rich and Thin Coconut Milk
2½ cups unsweetened shredded
    coconut
6 cups water

1. For Rich Coconut Milk, combine coconut and 3 cups of the water in large saucepan. Heat over medium heat, stirring occasionally, just to simmering. Remove from heat; let stand until lukewarm, 20 minutes.

2. Place sieve lined with dampened muslin cloth over large bowl. Process coconut mixture, half at a time, in blender 30 seconds; strain through sieve. Gather up edges of cloth, enclosing coconut; twist and squeeze firmly to extract all liquid.

3. Return coconut to saucepan. Transfer Rich Coconut Milk to small bowl or jar.

4. For Thin Coconut Milk, add remaining 3 cups water to coconut in pan; repeat Steps 1 and 2. Transfer Thin Coconut Milk to separate bowl or jar. *Makes about 2½ cups each Rich and Thin Coconut Milk*

Note: Coconut milk will keep for several days in refrigerator and up to 3 months in freezer.

# Rice with Chicken and Vegetables

(Takikomi Gohan)

2½ cups short-grain rice
  Cold water
4 medium dried black Chinese
  mushrooms
1½ cups hot water
1 large carrot
8 ounces boneless chicken breast
  (skinned, if desired)
2 pieces (about 3×6×¼ inches
  each) deep-fried tofu
3 cups boiling water
¼ cup saké
3 tablespoons plus 1 teaspoon soy
  sauce
2 teaspoons sugar
1 teaspoon salt
1 to 1½ cups water

1. Place rice in large bowl or pan; add cold water to cover. Stir rice gently with fingers several times (water will become cloudy or milky); drain rice in colander. Repeat washing and draining 3 or 4 times until water remains almost clear. Place rice in colander; drain 30 minutes.

2. Soak mushrooms in 1½ cups hot water in small bowl until tender, about 20 minutes. Remove mushrooms from bowl; squeeze slightly to extract water. Strain and reserve 1 cup of the soaking water. Remove and discard stems from mushrooms. Cut caps into ⅛- to ¼-inch-wide strips.

3. Cut carrot crosswise into 1-inch lengths; cut lengthwise into ⅛-inch-thick slices. Stack slices and cut lengthwise into ⅛-inch-wide strips. Cùt chicken into 1-inch squares.

4. Place tofu in sieve; pour boiling water slowly over tofu, turning to rinse both sides. Drain; pat dry with paper towels. Cut each piece in half lengthwise; cut each half crosswise into ¼-inch-wide strips.

5. Place reserved mushroom soaking liquid, 2 tablespoons saké, 3 tablespoons soy sauce, the sugar and salt in 3-quart saucepan; heat to boiling over medium-high heat. Add mushrooms and carrot pieces; boil gently 3 minutes. Add chicken and tofu; boil gently until chicken is cooked through, 4 to 6 minutes. Drain chicken mixture, reserving cooking liquid. Cover chicken mixture; keep warm.

6. Add enough water to reserved cooking liquid to bring amount to 2¾ cups liquid; place in heavy, 3-quart saucepan that has tight-fitting lid. Add remaining 2 tablespoons saké and 1 teaspoon soy sauce; stir in rice. Heat, covered, to full boiling over medium-high heat. Reduce heat to low; simmer, covered, until all liquid is absorbed, about 15 minutes. Do not lift lid during cooking. Remove from heat; let stand, covered, 15 minutes.

7. Gently fold chicken mixture into rice using wooden spoon or paddle. Lay dry kitchen towel over top of saucepan; cover towel with lid. Let stand 5 to 10 minutes to absorb excess moisture. Transfer to 4 individual serving bowls.          *Makes 4 servings*

2

2

4

7

7

# Rolled Sushi

(Nori-Maki)

2½ cups short-grain white rice
   Cold water
⅓ cup plus 1 tablespoon rice
   vinegar
2½ tablespoons sugar
1¾ teaspoons salt
3½ cups water
¼ cup natto (fermented beans)
5 tablespoons soy sauce
1 kyuri (Japanese cucumber)
   (about 6 ounces)
½ firm-ripe avocado, pared
6 sheets (7×8 inches) toasted nori
   (seaweed)
   Pickled ginger slices*

1. Place rice in large bowl; fill with cold water. Stir gently several times (water will become cloudy); drain rice in colander. Repeat washing and draining several times until water remains almost clear. Let rice drain in colander 1 hour.

2. Combine ⅓ cup of the vinegar, the sugar and salt in small saucepan. Heat over medium heat until sugar is dissolved. Remove from heat; let stand until cool.

3. Combine rice and 3 cups water in heavy, medium saucepan with tight-fitting lid. Heat, covered, over high heat to boiling. Reduce heat to low; simmer, covered, until all water has been absorbed, about 15 minutes. Do not lift lid during cooking.

4. Remove pan from heat. Quickly uncover pan; cover with clean towel, then with lid. Let stand 15 minutes.

5. Transfer rice to wide shallow nonmetal container; spread rice in even layer. Drizzle with cooled vinegar mixture; toss gently with folding motion using wet large wooden spoon or paddle until well mixed.

6. Continue tossing gently with one hand while fanning rice (using piece of cardboard, for example) with other hand, until rice cools to room temperature, about 10 minutes. Rice can be prepared ahead to this point; let stand at room temperature, covered with damp cloth, up to 4 hours. Do not refrigerate.

7. Mince natto; mix with 1 tablespoon of the soy sauce in small bowl. Cut kyuri in half lengthwise; reserve one half for another recipe. Cut remaining half into ⅓×⅓-inch strips. Cut avocado into ⅓×⅓-inch strips.

8. Using scissors, cut nori sheets in half crosswise. Mix remaining ½ cup water and 1 tablespoon vinegar in small bowl; this mixture is called tezu (hand vinegar) and is used to moisten hands when handling rice to prevent sticking.

9. Place half-sheet of nori, shiny side down, crosswise on bamboo sushi mat and 1 inch in from edge of mat closest to you. Moisten hands with tezu. Place ½ cup rice on nori; using hands, spread rice in even layer to cover all but ¾ inch of nori farthest from you. Spread 2 teaspoons of the natto mixture lengthwise in even row across center of rice.

10. Bring front edge of mat (and nori) up and over natto to form roll; continue rolling nori, using mat as a frame, so that empty edge of nori overlaps to form seam. Press mat firmly around roll to form even cylinder; hold in place 10 seconds to seal. Unroll mat and remove sushi roll. Repeat to form 4 natto-filled rolls in all.

11. Repeat directions in Step 9 to make 4 rolls with a cucumber strip in center. Then repeat procedure to make 4 rolls filled with an avocado strip.

12. Cut each sushi roll crosswise into 6 even pieces with very sharp knife; wipe knife clean and dip in tezu before each cut. Arrange Rolled Sushi on serving plate; garnish with pickled ginger slices arranged in flower shape. Serve with remaining soy sauce for dipping.    *Makes 8 servings (about 9 pieces each)*

Note: Other fillings suitable for Rolled Sushi include strips of fresh raw tuna or salmon, strips of cooked carrot or fresh shiitake mushrooms.

*Available in Oriental grocery stores.

5

6

9

10

10

# Pilaf with Cashews and Raisins

2 cups basamati or long-grain
    white rice (about 12 ounces)
    Cold water
1 tablespoon boiling water
1 gram dried saffron threads
5 cups water
2 teaspoons salt
2 pieces (2 inches each) cinnamon
    stick
5 whole cardamom pods
5 whole cloves
2 star anise
2 tablespoons rose water
2 drops yellow food coloring
½ cup melted Ghee (see page 74) or
    butter
½ cup golden raisins
¼ cup fresh mint leaves
⅔ cup toasted cashews
    Fresh mint sprig

1. Place rice in large bowl; fill with cold water. Stir gently several times (water will become cloudy); drain rice in colander. Repeat washing and draining several times until water remains almost clear. Let rice drain in colander.

2. Pour 1 tablespoon boiling water over saffron in cup; let soak at least 10 minutes.

3. Combine rice and 5 cups water in Dutch oven; heat over high heat to boiling. Add salt, cinnamon, cardamom, cloves and star anise; stir gently. Cook, covered, over low heat, 7 minutes.

4. Drain rice; return to pan. Cook, covered, over very low heat, 5 minutes; remove from heat.

5. Mix rose water and food coloring in small cup; add saffron and its soaking liquid.

6. Drizzle Ghee over rice by holding small sieve over rice and moving it in circular motion while pouring Ghee through sieve. Repeat procedure, drizzling food coloring liquid over rice. Sprinkle saffron threads on top of rice. Do not stir rice.

7. Wrap lid of pan with damp kitchen towel; place on pan. Place heavy object on top of lid to weigh it down. Cook rice over very low heat, 30 minutes.

8. Turn heat off. Sprinkle raisins and mint leaves on top of rice; do not stir. Let stand, covered, 5 minutes.

9. Stir rice gently to mix white and colored portions. Remove whole spices, reserving 1 cinnamon stick for garnish if desired. Transfer rice to serving dish; sprinkle with cashews. Garnish with cinnamon stick and mint sprig; serve immediately. *Makes 6 to 8 servings*

5

6

7

# Indonesian Fried Rice

(Nasi Goreng)

1⅓ cups long-grain white rice (not converted)
2⅓ cups water
2 ounces shallots
3 to 4 hot fresh red chili peppers, seeded
2 cloves garlic
1 teaspoon salt
¼ cup plus 2 tablespoons vegetable oil
1 tablespoon Fried Onion Flakes (see page 35)
4 to 6 large eggs
2 romaine lettuce leaves
1 cucumber, pared and sliced
1 large tomato, sliced

1. Rinse rice thoroughly in sieve under cold running water; drain well. Combine rice and water in medium saucepan. Heat, covered, over medium heat to boiling. Reduce heat to low; cook, covered, until water is absorbed and rice is firm-tender, 10 to 12 minutes.

2. Transfer rice to large bowl; stir with fork to loosen and separate grains. Let stand, uncovered, until completely cool. (Cooled rice can be refrigerated, covered, overnight; bring to room temperature before proceeding with recipe.)

3. Grind shallots, chili peppers, garlic and salt in mortar with pestle or in blender to coarse paste.

4. Heat ¼ cup of the oil in wok over high heat until hot, about 30 seconds. Add shallot paste. Reduce heat to medium; stir-fry 4 minutes.

5. Add rice; stir-fry, tossing and breaking up clumps of rice, until rice is well fried and grains are separated and evenly coated with shallot paste, 6 to 8 minutes. Transfer to serving dish; sprinkle with Fried Onion Flakes.

6. Heat remaining 2 tablespoons oil in large skillet over medium heat. Break eggs into skillet; fry, turning once, until done to taste. Arrange eggs on top of rice.

7. Garnish rice with lettuce and some of the cucumber and tomato slices. Serve immediately with remaining cucumber and tomato.

*Makes 4 to 6 servings*

# EGGS & TOFU

# Tofu Custard

6 ounces tofu, rinsed
¾ cup plus ⅓ cup chicken broth
8 ounces fresh oyster mushrooms
    (or 15-ounce can straw
    mushrooms, rinsed and
    drained)
4 or 5 round slices Canadian bacon
    or ham (3 to 4 ounces)
4 large egg whites
½ cup milk
1¼ teaspoons salt
⅛ teaspoon white pepper
    Boiling water
2 tablespoons peanut oil
¾ cup fresh broccoli florets
¼ cup plus 2 teaspoons cold water
1 teaspoon cornstarch

1. Crumble tofu coarsely; press between several layers of paper towels to remove excess moisture. Combine tofu and ⅓ cup broth in blender container; puree until smooth.

2. Trim root ends of mushrooms; break into small clusters. Arrange mushrooms in a border near edge of heatproof dish about 9 inches in diameter and 1 inch deep. Cut bacon slices in half crosswise; arrange upright and overlapping in a circle inside the mushroom border.

3. Beat egg whites very lightly in medium bowl; gently whisk in tofu mixture until smooth. Add milk, ¾ teaspoon salt and the pepper; stir with whisk until thoroughly mixed.

4. Pour tofu mixture into center of prepared dish. Use as much of the custard as will fit without flowing over ham slices. Place dish in steamer. Spread clean thin kitchen towel over steamer; cover with lid.

4

5. Place steamer in wok; add boiling water to wok to level of 1 inch below steamer. Adjust heat for steady, gentle steam (about medium). Steam custard just until knife inserted in center is withdrawn clean, about 10 minutes. Remove steamer from wok; empty wok and wipe dry.

6. Heat wok over high heat 15 seconds; add oil and heat until hot, about 30 seconds. Add broccoli; stir-fry 1 minute. Add ¼ cup water; cover and steam-cook until crisp-tender, about 30 seconds. Remove broccoli; drain on paper towels. Dry wok.

8

7. Heat remaining ¾ cup broth and ½ teaspoon salt in wok over high heat to boiling; reduce heat to medium. Mix cornstarch and 2 teaspoons cold water in a cup until smooth; add to wok. Cook and stir until sauce thickens, about 1 minute.

8. Remove dish from steamer; blot water around edge of dish with paper towels. Arrange broccoli in center of custard.

9

9. Gently ladle about ½ of sauce over custard to cover with a thin film. Serve custard immediately with remaining sauce, if desired.     *Makes 4 servings*

EGGS AND TOFU   181

# Savory Steamed Egg Custard

(Chawan-Mushi)

2½ cups Dashi (see page 48)
4 teaspoons saké
2½ teaspoons light soy sauce
1 teaspoon salt
6 ounces boneless skinless chicken
8 medium shrimp, in shells
4 medium or 8 small fresh black
    Chinese mushrooms
1 small carrot
2 ounces fresh spinach, washed,
    well drained
¼ cup water
1 piece (1 inch square) lemon rind
4 large eggs
3 to 4 cups boiling water

1. Heat Dashi, 1 tablespoon saké, 1½ teaspoons soy sauce and the salt in the 1-quart saucepan over medium-high heat until hot; stir to dissolve salt. Cool completely.

2. Cut chicken into 1-inch squares; place in small bowl. Stir in remaining 1 teaspoon saké and 1 teaspoon soy sauce; let stand 10 minutes. Drain.

3. Shell each shrimp, leaving tail and section of shell nearest tail attached. Remove veins. Remove and discard mushroom stems; if using medium mushrooms, cut caps into halves. Cut carrot crosswise into ⅛-inch-thick slice; if desired, cut slice into halves or quarters.

4. Place spinach and ¼ cup water in 1-quart saucepan; heat to boiling over high heat. Reduce heat to medium; simmer 2 minutes. Drain. Cut spinach into 1-inch lengths.

5. Cut lemon rind into ¹⁄₁₆-inch-wide strips; reserve.

6. Mix eggs well with fork in large bowl; do not beat. Stir Dashi mixture gently into eggs in slow, steady stream. Strain egg mixture through fine sieve or cheesecloth.

7. Place chicken, shrimp, mushrooms, carrot and spinach in 4 individual custard bowls, dividing evenly. (Use heatproof coffee cups or mugs, if desired.) Ladle ¼ of the egg mixture into each bowl, leaving at least ½-inch space at top of each bowl. Cover each bowl with aluminum foil.

8. Place boiling water to a depth of about 1 inch in steamer (or large kettle); set bowls in steamer basket (or on rack above water). Cover steamer with vented lid (or position kettle lid so small amount of steam can escape). Place steamer over medium-high heat 1 minute; reduce heat and adjust to maintain steady, gentle steam. Steam until wooden pick inserted in custard comes out clean, 15 to 20 minutes. Carefully remove bowls from steamer. Serve hot, garnished with lemon strips.          *Makes 4 servings*

6

6

7

# Stir-Fried Eggs and Pork

3 ounces canned bamboo shoots, rinsed and drained
3 ounces fresh spinach, washed, well drained
⅛ ounce dried cloud ears, washed, well drained
6 ounces boneless pork shoulder
4 teaspoons rice wine
3½ teaspoons cornstarch
1 teaspoon sesame oil
2 tablespoons cold water
1½ teaspoons soy sauce
1 tablespoon Chinese black vinegar
1½ teaspoons sugar
5 large eggs
5 tablespoons peanut oil
3 tablespoons finely chopped green onion
2 teaspoons minced pared fresh ginger root
1 clove garlic, minced
½ to 1 teaspoon chili sauce with soybean

1. Cut bamboo shoots into ¹⁄₁₆-inch-thick slices; cut slices into 2×1-inch pieces. Cut spinach leaves crosswise into 2-inch pieces. Break cloud ears into 1-inch pieces.

2. Cut pork across the grain into ⅛-inch-thick slices; cut slices into 2×1-inch pieces. Combine pork and 1½ teaspoons rice wine in small bowl. Stir in 1½ teaspoons cornstarch; mix well. Stir in sesame oil. Marinate at room temperature 30 minutes.

3. Mix 2 teaspoons cornstarch and the cold water in cup until smooth; stir in soy sauce, vinegar, sugar and remaining 2½ teaspoons rice wine. Beat eggs in medium bowl.

4. Heat wok over high heat 15 seconds; add 2 tablespoons peanut oil and heat until hot, about 30 seconds. Add eggs; quickly swirl around wok. As eggs begin to puff at edges, push cooked portion to one side, tilting wok in opposite direction, letting uncooked portion flow down. Repeat until eggs are set, not hard. (Work quickly; total cooking time for eggs is about 20 seconds.) Transfer to plate. Chop eggs with spatula into ½-inch-wide strips.

5. Add remaining 3 tablespoons peanut oil to wok; heat over high heat until hot. Scatter in pork; stir-fry until no longer pink, 1 minute. Add onion, ginger and garlic; stir-fry 10 seconds. Stir in chili sauce; stir-fry 5 seconds. Add cloud ears and bamboo shoots; stir-fry 30 seconds.

6. Stir soy sauce mixture; add to wok. Cook and stir until thickened, 15 seconds. Stir in spinach. Add eggs; cook and stir until eggs are heated through, about 10 seconds.

*Makes 3 to 4 servings*

1
2
5

# Ma-Po Bean Curd

1 tablespoon Szechuan
    peppercorns
12 to 14 ounces bean curd, drained
¾ cup chicken broth
1 tablespoon soy sauce
1 tablespoon dry sherry
2 teaspoons minced fresh ginger
    root
2 cloves garlic, minced
1 tablespoon hot bean sauce
2 tablespoons vegetable oil
4 ounces lean ground pork
2 green onions, thinly sliced
1½ tablespoons cornstarch
3 tablespoons water
1 teaspoon sesame oil

1. Toast peppercorns in small dry skillet over medium-low heat, stirring constantly, until fragrant, about 2 minutes. Transfer to plate; let cool. Pound peppercorns in mortar with pestle.

2. Cut bean curd into ½-inch cubes.

3. Combine chicken broth, soy sauce and sherry in small bowl.

4. Combine ginger, garlic and hot bean sauce in small bowl.

5. Heat vegetable oil in wok or large skillet over high heat until hot. Add pork; cook and stir, breaking pork into small pieces, until it is no longer pink, about 2 minutes. Add hot bean sauce mixture. Stir-fry until meat absorbs color from bean sauce, about 1 minute.

6. Add chicken broth mixture and bean curd to wok. Reduce heat to low; simmer, uncovered, 5 minutes. Stir in onions. Blend cornstarch and water in small cup until smooth. Add to wok; cook, stirring constantly, until sauce boils and thickens slightly. Stir in sesame oil. Pass ground peppercorns separately to sprinkle over each serving. *Makes 3 to 4 servings*

1             1             3

# Fresh Tofu with Condiments

(Hiyayakko)

3 or 4 green onions
3 green shiso leaves
4 teaspoons soy sauce
1 pound tofu, drained
¼ cup dried bonito flakes
2 tablespoons grated pared fresh
    ginger root

1. Cut green onions into ⅛-inch-thick slices. Remove stems from shiso; cut lengthwise into ½-inch-wide strips. Stack strips; cut crosswise into ¹⁄₁₆-inch-wide strips.

2. Place 1 teaspoon soy sauce in each of 4 small bowls for dipping sauce.

3. Cut tofu into pieces, approximately 1½×3×1 inches. Place about ¼ of the tofu in each of 4 serving bowls.

4. Sprinkle shiso, green onions and bonito flakes over tofu, dividing evenly. Place 1½ teaspoons ginger next to tofu in each bowl. Serve, dipping tofu briefly in soy sauce, as desired. *Makes 4 servings*

# Tofu Saute
### (Abura-Yakidofu)

1¼ pounds tofu, drained
2 medium fresh black Chinese mushrooms
1 medium carrot
1 small potato
1 cup cold water
1 small green bell pepper
4 to 6 ounces tiny shrimp, shelled (deveined, if desired)
1 large egg white
¼ cup plus 1 teaspoon soy sauce
1 tablespoon saké
¼ teaspoon salt
6 tablespoons cornstarch
2 teaspoons rice vinegar
2 tablespoons vegetable oil

1. Cut tofu horizontally into ⅜-inch slices. Press with dry paper towels to remove moisture; repeat several times.

2. Remove and discard stems from mushrooms. Cut caps into halves or quarters; cut halves into ¹⁄₁₆-inch-wide slices. Cut carrot crosswise into 1-inch lengths; cut lengthwise into ¹⁄₁₆-inch-thick slices. Stack slices and cut into ¹⁄₁₆-inch-wide strips.

3. Pare potato; cut crosswise into ¹⁄₁₆-inch-thick slices. Stack slices and cut into ¹⁄₁₆-inch-wide strips. Place in the cold water in small bowl; soak 5 minutes. Drain. Cut green pepper lengthwise into 1-inch-wide strips; cut crosswise into ¹⁄₁₆-inch-wide strips.

4. Mix mushroom, carrot, potato, green pepper, shrimp, egg white, 1 teaspoon soy sauce, the saké and salt in medium bowl. Sprinkle ¼ cup cornstarch over shrimp mixture; stir to mix well.

5. Lay tofu flat on work surface; sieve one side of tofu slices with remaining 2 tablespoons cornstarch. Spread shrimp mixture evenly on tofu slices; layer of shrimp mixture should be about ½-inch thick. Press mixture lightly.

6. For sauce, mix remaining ¼ cup soy sauce and the rice vinegar in small bowl; reserve.

7. Heat 1 tablespoon oil in 12-inch skillet over high heat. Add tofu, shrimp side down; saute until light brown, 3 to 4 minutes. Carefully turn tofu slices over, using large spatula. Add remaining 1 tablespoon oil to skillet; saute tofu until light brown, 2 or 3 minutes longer.

8. Carefully cut tofu slices crosswise into 2 or 3 pieces, if desired. Transfer to platter or individual serving plates; pour reserved sauce over tofu. Serve immediately. *Makes 4 to 5 servings*

# Seasoned Fish and Tofu

¾ pound skinless firm white fish
 fillets, such as cod, haddock or
 sea bass
2½ tablespoons rice wine
 ¼ teaspoon salt
 1 large egg white, lightly beaten
 3 tablespoons cornstarch
 1 pound tofu
1¼ cups chicken broth
 2 tablespoons soy sauce
 2 teaspoons Chinese black vinegar
 2 teaspoons sugar
 1 teaspoon sesame oil
 2 tablespoons cold water
 3 cups vegetable oil
 3 tablespoons peanut oil
 2 teaspoons minced pared fresh
 ginger root
 1 clove garlic, minced
 1 to 2 teaspoons chili paste with
 garlic
 3 tablespoons finely chopped
 green onion

1. Cut fish crosswise into ½-inch-wide strips; cut strips into 1½-inch lengths. Combine fish, 1 tablespoon rice wine and the salt in medium bowl. Stir in egg white. Sprinkle with 5 teaspoons cornstarch; stir until smooth. Refrigerate, covered, 30 minutes to 1 hour.

2. Cut tofu into ⅜-inch-thick slices; cut slices into 2×¾-inch pieces. Mix chicken broth, soy sauce, vinegar, sugar, sesame oil and remaining 1½ tablespoons rice wine in small bowl. Mix 4 teaspoons cornstarch with the water in a cup until smooth.

3. Heat wok over high heat 20 seconds; add vegetable oil to wok and heat to 325°F. Stir fish to separate. Fry fish, ½ at a time, just until cooked through, 1½ to 2 minutes. Remove with strainer; drain on paper towels. Reheat oil to 325°F and repeat with remaining fish. Remove oil from wok; wipe clean.

4. Heat large saucepan of water to boiling. Add tofu. Heat to boiling; reduce heat to low. Simmer tofu 2 minutes; drain thoroughly.

5. Heat wok over high heat 15 seconds; add peanut oil and heat until hot, about 30 seconds. Reduce heat to medium; stir-fry ginger and garlic 10 seconds. Stir in chili paste; stir-fry 5 seconds. Add broth mixture, tofu and green onion.

6. Increase heat to high; heat to boiling. Reduce heat to medium-low; simmer uncovered, stirring gently, 4 minutes. Stir in fish; simmer and stir 1 minute. Quickly stir cornstarch mixture and add to wok; cook and stir gently until sauce thickens and coats ingredients, 30 to 45 seconds. Serve immediately. *Makes 4 servings*

2     3     5     6     7

# Tofu with Chicken and Vegetables

(Iridofu)

4 medium dried black Chinese
   mushrooms
   Boiling water
10 ounces tofu, drained
1 piece (3 inches) carrot (about
   1 inch in diameter)
4 green onions
2 tablespoons soy sauce
1 tablespoon sugar
1 tablespoon vegetable oil
4 ounces ground chicken (about
   1 cup)
1 cube (½ inch) pared fresh ginger
   root, minced
1½ tablespoons saké
1 large egg, well mixed

1. Soak mushrooms in the boiling water until tender, about 20 minutes; drain. Remove and discard stems from mushrooms. Cut caps into halves; cut halves crosswise into ¹⁄₁₆-inch-thick slices.

2. Place tofu in sieve over medium bowl. Using fork, crumble tofu coarsely; drain.

3. Cut carrot in half lengthwise; cut halves lengthwise into ¹⁄₁₆-inch-thick slices. Stack slices and cut into ¹⁄₁₆-inch-wide strips. Cut green onions into ½-inch lengths.

4. Mix soy sauce and sugar in small bowl; stir to dissolve sugar. Reserve.

5. Heat oil in 2-quart saucepan over high heat. Add chicken; saute, stirring constantly, 3 minutes. Add ginger, carrot and mushrooms to chicken; saute, stirring constantly, until carrot is tender, 2 to 3 minutes.

6. Add tofu to chicken mixture; cook, stirring gently, until tofu is hot, 1 to 2 minutes. Pour saké over chicken mixture; cook and stir 1 minute.

7. Stir in soy-sauce mixture and egg; cook, stirring gently, until egg is soft-set, 1 to 2 minutes. Add onions; stir to mix well. Serve immediately or cool to room temperature.

*Makes 4 servings*

# INDEX